ST. RITA
SAINT OF THE IMPOSSIBLE

Image of St. Rita venerated in the chapel of the
Annunciation at Nice.

ST. RITA
SAINT OF THE IMPOSSIBLE

PRAYERS AND DEVOTIONS TO ST. RITA
INCLUDING THE DEVOTION OF
THE FIFTEEN THURSDAYS

———

**With
A Short Life of This Great Saint
and Prayerful Reflections upon It**

Illustrated

CATHOLIC BOOK PUBLISHING CORP.
New Jersey

NIHIL OBSTAT: Francis J. McAree, S.T.D.
Censor Librorum

IMPRIMATUR: ✠ Patrick J. Sheridan, D.D.
Vicar General, Archdiocese of New York

The Nihil Obstat and Imprimatur are official declarations that a book or a pamphlet is free of doctrinal or moral error. No implication is contained therein that those who have granted the Nihil Obstat and Imprimatur agree with the contents, opinions, or statements expressed.

The material in this book originally appeared in the French prayer book *Prières de Chaque Jour: Les Quinze Jeudis de Sainte Rita* published by Oeuvres de Sainte Rita, Nice. The English translation is by Rev. John Otto.

The text (with slight changes) of the Mass of St. Rita in the Appendix has been reproduced with permission from the *Augustinian Missal* © 1979 by the English Speaking Provinces of the Order of Saint Augustine. All rights reserved.

(T-128)

© 1999 Catholic Book Publishing Corp., N.J.

Printed in Canada   5 6 7 8 9 10

PREFACE

FROM time immemorial Catholics have been devoted to the Saints of God. In the words of the early Christians of Smyrna: "We adore Christ because He is the Son of God; we love the Saints because they are disciples and imitators of our Lord."

Since the Saints lived the Christian life to the full, we seek from them an example in their way of life, fellowship in their communion, and aid by their intercession.

Because of our union with Christ we are united with all those who share His life in the larger family of God, the Communion of Saints. We on earth, members of the Church Militant, still fighting the good fight as soldiers of Christ, still journeying on our way to our Father's house, are helped by the prayers and encouragement of the victorious and blessed members of the family, the Church Triumphant in heaven. We honor the Saints and endeavor to imitate the example of their virtuous lives.

We manifest the love and unity that are ours in the Communion of Saints also by praying to the Saints in heaven as our patrons and intercessors with God. Not only is their intercession with God very powerful because of the love they have shown Him on earth, but we also share in their merits gained by their heroic life.

One of the Saints whose aid has been most sought over the course of the last five hundred years has been St. Rita of Cascia. Christians have been fascinated by her life and have called upon the help of her intercession with God. So great has been her response that she has become known as the "Saint of the Impossible."

This book includes Rita's *Life,* in accord with the words of the Second Vatican Council:

"When we look at the lives of those who have faithfully followed Christ, we are inspired for seeking the City that is to come. At the same time, we are shown a safe path by which among the vicissitudes of this world and in keeping with our state in life we will be able to arrive at perfect union with Christ, that is, perfect holiness" *(Constitution on the Church,* no. 50).

Interwoven among the events of that life are a series of *Reflections* upon it that can guide our spiritual life as well as *Prayers* that call upon her powerful intercession with God on our behalf.

Also included are a series of *Novenas, Triduums, and Prayers* by which one can request St. Rita's intercession in various situations.

The *Appendix* contains the texts for the Mass of St. Rita. In this way, readers may utilize them as prayers on her feast day and on any other day.

May this book make St. Rita better known and loved and thus bring Christians closer to Christ. At the same time, may it help provide relief through the aid of St. Rita for all who need help in their life situation.

CONTENTS

THE FIFTEEN THURSDAYS OF ST. RITA

Origin and Spiritual Value..11
Preparatory Prayer To Be Recited Every Thursday at the
    Beginning of Each Exercise 13

First Thursday

Life: Rita . . . or the Precious "Pearl" in a Desolate Land 14
Reflection: The Value of Saints in Our Lives 15
Prayer: For a Return to the Evangelical Life......................................16

Second Thursday

Life: The Miracle of the Bees 18
Reflection: Blessed Are the Meek..20
Prayer: For the Spirit of Meekness 21

Third Thursday

Life: Education by Image and Example...22
Reflection: Importance of a Catholic Education 23
Prayer: To Ensure the Religious Education of Our Children..............25

Fourth Thursday

Life: A Dreaded Marriage That Turns Out Well 27
Reflection: Example of Heroic Patience 29
Prayer: For Those in Troubled Marriages...30

Fifth Thursday

Life: Home Life and the Service of Others..32
Reflection: The Need for Penance 33
Prayer: To Foster Mortification and Sacrifice 35

Sixth Thursday

Life: Two Severe Trials: Deaths of Parents and Husband.................37
Reflection: The Danger of Sudden Death 38
Prayer: To Obtain the Christian Meaning of Death.........................40

Seventh Thursday

Life: A Christian Mother...42
Reflection: Forgiveness of Others 44
Prayer: To Practice True Charity 45
Prayer with St. Rita..46

Eighth Thursday

Life: Knocking at the Convent Door......................................47
Reflection: Be Reconciled with One Another 49
Prayer: To Obtain the Gift of Reconciliation 50

Ninth Thursday

Life: The Miracle of the Vine 52
Reflection: Poverty, Chastity, and Obedience 54
Prayer: To Practice the Evangelical Virtues 56

Tenth Thursday

Life: The Stigmata of the Crown of Thorns...............................58
Reflection: Focusing on Christ's Passion 60
Prayer: To Obtain True Contrition.......................................62

Eleventh Thursday

Life: The Roman Jubilee...63
Reflection: The Value of Pilgrimages 66
Prayer: To Fix Our Eyes on Heaven during Our Earthly Pilgrimage....67

Twelfth Thursday

Life: Days as a Recluse 69
Reflection: The Contribution of Contemplatives 71
Prayer: To Discover What God Expects of Us 72

Thirteenth Thursday

Life: Final Miracles—Roses and Figs.................................74
Reflection: The Need To Produce Worthy Fruits of Charity...............75
Prayer: To See Christ in Others 77

Fourteenth Thursday

Life: The True Day of Birth 79
Reflection: The Right Idea about Death 80
Prayer: To Prepare for a Good Death 82

Fifteenth Thursday

Life: The Vine in Flower Has Spread Its Perfume.......................84
Reflection: The School of the Saints 87
Prayer: To Imitate St. Rita in Bearing Witness to Christ 89
Prayer to St. Rita 91

NOVENAS, TRIDUUMS, AND PRAYERS TO ST. RITA

Reasons Why Our Prayers Are Pleasing to the Lord 93
Novena to St. Rita 95
Alternative Novena to St. Rita 99
Short Novena to St. Rita 102
Triduum in Honor of St. Rita: To Obtain a Grace......................103
Triduum in Honor of St. Rita: For the Sick 105
Triduum in Honor of St. Rita: To Give Thanks 108
Prayer in Difficult and Desperate Cases 111
Prayer of Thanksgiving 113
Supplication to St. Rita 115
Litany of St. Rita 116
Prayer for a Particular Grace 118
Prayer for a Sick Person...119
St. Rita's Roses—Prayer of the Roses 120

APPENDIX

Mass of St. Rita...121

St. Rita's altar in the Chapel of the
Annunciation at Nice.

THE FIFTEEN THURSDAYS OF ST. RITA

ORIGIN AND SPIRITUAL VALUE

BEFORE beginning the devotion of the Fifteen Thursdays of St. Rita, it seems necessary to give some explanations concerning its origin and import. That will help to spread its pious exercise among followers of St. Rita and, among people generally, will help increase the number of good and meritorious works.

It was certainly a very singular gift, the gift of the thorn, that the crucified Jesus made to His faithful servant, St. Rita. She welcomed it and kept it as the seal of her love and passion for her Divine Bride. She wore it during the last fifteen years of her life, till death.

The practice of the Fifteen Thursdays preceding the feast of St. Rita was begun in remembrance of those fifteen years. It can be said that today, in places where St. Rita is venerated, there is not a church or chapel in which this practice is not carried out in private or in groups.

At Cascia, in its church, and at Nice, in the Chapel of the Annunciation, St. Rita is venerated in a very special way. Large crowds attend the devotion, and solemnity reigns.

This pious practice, which has spread far and wide, ought to inspire the faithful to receive the Sacraments of Penance and the

Eucharist and to live a Christian life. It ought further to inspire them to pray, meditate, and do works of piety. Above all, this devotion should lead those who practice it to learn more about the mystery of the crucified Christ and His Passion, of which St. Rita received a mark in a supernatural way on her forehead.

PREPARATORY PRAYER

TO BE RECITED EVERY THURSDAY AT THE BEGINNING OF EACH EXERCISE

O my God,
Whose splendor fills heaven and earth,
I believe You are present here.
I know You are near me and in me.
Immersed in my unworthiness,
I deeply adore You.

I thank You for the many graces
You have accorded me
and for all the graces, spiritual and material,
You in Your fatherly goodness have prepared
to strengthen my weakness.

I ask You to forgive the many faults
I have committed in the past.
I beg the help of Your grace
to keep me from offending You in the future
and to remain faithful to the promises
I have made to You many times.
I sincerely renew them today.

O Blessed Virgin, Saints in heaven,
and especially you, St. Rita,
help me make this Holy Exercise devoutly
in order to obtain the light of mind
and the strength of will
to attain my eternal salvation.
Amen.

FIRST THURSDAY

Preparatory Prayer, p. 13

LIFE: RITA . . . OR THE PRECIOUS "PEARL" IN A DESOLATE LAND

RITA is a lovely name. It comes from the Latin "margarita," which means "pearl." It was a providential name, seeing that in the fifteenth century St. Rita was one of the most precious jewels of Holy Church. She lived five hundred years ago, at the time of St. Joan of Arc. When Joan was burned in Rouen, our Saint was probably about fifty years old.

In France there was a war that lasted a hundred years, the frightful rivalry between the Gasconians and the Burgundians. In Italy things were no better, as the Guelphs were in conflict with the Ghibellines. The Guelphs were for the Pope, the Ghibellines for the Emperor.

At Rita's birth, the Church herself was divided. The "Great Schism" had begun three years earlier. For forty years there were two Popes opposed to each other and even three at the end.

The Mohammedans profited. Four years before Rita's death they took Constantinople, and they spoke of nothing less than feeding their horses in the Basilica of St. Peter in Rome.

Everywhere there was shameless debauchery. The clergy themselves were very lax. Joan of Arc's trial was evidence of that.

It was then that God raised up a chosen soul, a truly precious "Pearl" in this desolate land.

Cascia was a small territorial district of Italy, situated in the Apennines. One of its hamlets was called Roccaporena. There Rita was born, the Saint we love.

REFLECTION: THE VALUE OF SAINTS IN OUR LIVES

*I*F *the Church of Jesus Christ is holy, one reason is that she has produced Saints in every age. Saints are the lightning rod of the world. Happily for us, we are not isolated individuals. We form an immense body called the "Mystical Body" of Christ. All of us are members.*

In this Body there are many ways of behavior, some good and some not so good.

Among us there is a "common union" called the "Communion of Saints," a union of all baptized people. If all lived up to their Baptism, that would be wonderful. Regrettably, in this large "Body" there are many spiritually sick members, who weaken the whole.

This weakness must be restrengthened. And it is the Saints who are the ones charged with this function. By their merits they enable the Body to live in a more holy fashion. They also have a hand in keeping the world in existence. We ought to acknowledge what they do and, above all, thank them for it. Our first attitude

*toward them should therefore be an attitude of
acknowledgment and our first prayer a prayer
of praise and thanksgiving.*

*Not only are Saints the counterbalance to
the sins of the world; they are also witnesses of
the Gospel. Their existence is like a living lesson for all to see. They show us the human
masterpiece that can be achieved by following
Christ and taking His message and counsels
seriously.*

*This is what St. Rita did: take the message
seriously. In a century that was particularly
callous, with some others like St. Joan of Arc,
for example, she helped to save the people of
her time: she showed them the way of the
supernatural.*

*The first thing we should ask of her is to save
us also and help us break away from whatever
is irreligious in our daily life. We should moreover ask her to show us how we must change if
we are to be really Christian.*

PRAYER: FOR A RETURN TO THE
EVANGELICAL LIFE

O St. Rita,
the Providence of God raised you up
in the fifteenth century
to help save the Christian world
from the lamentable state
in which it had fallen.

Look at our times.
They are scarcely any better.
Now and then we too are divided
by so much misunderstanding
and, at times, hatred.
For us also the peril is at our door
because of our sins.
By your merits,
keep away from us and our children
the frightful dangers of war.

Our misery consists above all
in being so far removed from true Christianity.
Help us to return to a life.
that is more in harmony with the Gospels.
By your example,
make us understand that we must be converted
and live in charity as true baptized people
of Christ Jesus.
Amen.

SECOND THURSDAY

Preparatory Prayer, p. 13

LIFE: THE MIRACLE OF THE BEES

THE father of our Saint was Antonio Lotti, and her mother was Amy Ferri. Little is known about them beyond the fact of their reputation for goodness, and that is enormous, especially at a time like theirs when the small villages were painfully divided. Roccaporena was one of the villages.

Antonio and Amy had no stake in the political quarrels that set Guelphs against Ghibellines. On the contrary, they sought to calm spirits and rivalries, so much so that they were nicknamed the "conciliators" or the "peace-bearers" of Jesus Christ. Their daughter would learn from them.

But over the years a secret sorrow disturbed their tranquil joy. They had no children. In their home none of the cries that awaken so many echoes in the heart of parents had yet been heard. Many times they had, to this end, addressed to God the most ardent prayers.

Just when everything had led them to believe that God wanted the sacrifice of this legitimate desire, the unexpected happened, recalling the wondrous event that took place at the birth of John the Baptist, the precursor of Jesus. To spouses advanced in age God sent offspring, in this instance a baby girl. It was probably the year 1381.

"Margarita" was the name given the baby at its Baptism in the Church of St. Mary of the Commoners in Cascia. The name "Rita," under which she was canonized, is a diminutive of the Italian "Margarita." Even in the convent she was "Sister Rita." Today still she is known and venerated in the whole world by this dimunitive.

Tradition has it that one day the little girl was put in a wicker basket and placed under a shade tree so her parents could go work in the fields. A swarm of bees appeared and surrounded her. They entered the mouth of the child and, without stinging her, deposited their honey.

A harvester happened to pass by. He had gashed his hand and was returning to the village to have it taken care of. Seeing the swarm, he made a motion with the wounded hand to drive them away. Suddenly the hand was healed. The episode made a deep impression on the good people of Roccaporena. The memory of it has been transmitted to posterity by a fresco that adorns the little chapel built on the very spot of the miracle.

The Church herself spoke of the event in the lessons of the *Roman Breviary.*

As for the bees, they followed Rita. After five hundred years bees still live on the grounds of the convent in Cascia. In the seventeenth century Pope Urban VIII asked that some be brought to him in Rome. He took one of them, tied a silken thread around it, and let it escape. It returned to Cascia, or so it is said.

Today still, a touch of mystery hangs over these bees of St. Rita's convent. They are a little larger than ordinary bees and have neither stinger nor feeler. Eleven months of the year they remain shut up in the holes of an old wall. The week of the Passion they come out of their holes and always return to them during the octave of the feast of the Saint.

We should regard this tradition—more than as a historical fact—as symbol of what this infant would be: sweet and industrious.

REFLECTION: BLESSED ARE THE MEEK

*R*ITA *was to be a Saint of meekness. She had, so to speak, been predestined to it by the goodness of her parents. In the midst of much cruelty they were the "conciliators" of Jesus Christ. They worked to put an end to all the hatred in the village of Roccaporena.*

The parents of Rita took the beatitude about "peacemakers" seriously. Note that this word means: those who "make" peace, who are its artisans: "Blessed are the peacemakers, for they shall be called children of God" (Matthew 5:9).

And we, are we artisans of peace wherever we are: at home, at work, or anywhere else? How do we handle our relations with one another? It would do us no good to have a certain piety if at the same time we were like people who deliberately create misunderstanding and, as the saying goes, throw oil on the fire.

That Rita was predestined to be a Saint of meekness was also suggested, at the time of her infancy, by the delightful miracle of the bees. Honey has always been a symbol of meekness. Let us not forget St. Francis de Sales affirming, from experience, that more flies are caught with a spoonful of honey than with a barrel of vinegar.

Our Lord weighed His words well when He said: "Blessed are the meek, for they shall inherit the land" (Matthew 5:4).

PRAYER: FOR THE SPIRIT OF MEEKNESS

O St. Rita,
deeply Christian parents inculcated in you
the sense of Christian goodness.
Teach us to put it into practice.
Obtain for us the honey of meekness.

We know that to acquire this virtue
we must first be capable of mastering ourselves.
And we know very little about doing that.

We let ourselves be led by our antipathies,
our prejudices, our material interests.
Help us change all that,
you who were the Saint of meekness.
Amen.

THIRD THURSDAY

Preparatory Prayer, p. 13

LIFE: EDUCATION BY IMAGE AND EXAMPLE

WE know nothing very precise about the education the Lotti gave their daughter. They certainly did not make her a woman of learning. One simply cannot give what one does not have. At the time of the Lotti the poor were probably unlettered, as were many people of modest means. Besides, there was no school-house in Roccaporena.

The great book of images that children studied was the church of their village. Pictures, paintings, statues, stained glass windows, all helped to excite their minds and hearts. The land of Rita, Umbria, already was rich in native painters, who would soon give rise to the Peruginos and the Raphaels.

Child that she was, Rita did not have eyes enough for the many wonders mother Lotti explained to her. There were the Bible, especially the Gospel narratives. There was also the beautiful Golden Legend of the Saints and the legends of the Poverello, Francis of Assisi.

In the Bible and the legends Rita quenched her thirst for religious knowledge. One "book," nevertheless, topped them all: the Crucifix, the imposing Crucifix of so many Italian churches. It taught the child everything: love of Jesus, hatred of sin, and the spirit of penance.

Nothing, unfortunately, is known about the First Communion and the Confirmation of this exceptional child. However, we can surmise that each such occasion must have strengthened her sense of generosity.

Rita was the sole caretaker of her aged parents, and almost all the work around the house fell to her. As a reward her mother sometimes offered to buy her a small item she could use at her washstand. The little girl would graciously decline.

Like the monks living as solitaries in the caves around Roccaporena, the so-called Hermits of St. Augustine, Rita loved solitude. Her parents even let her have a small, secluded room. This she made over into a chapel decorated with images of the Passion. Here she prayed to Christ with all her heart, dreaming of becoming His bride by taking the veil of a nun.

We shall see the detour Providence allowed her to take before making this dream a reality.

REFLECTION: IMPORTANCE OF A CATHOLIC EDUCATION

*T*HERE *is a great difference between Rita's education and the education of most children today. Times have changed, for sure. In our day it would be unthinkable to let a child remain unlettered. Children need to be educated if they are to take their place in society.*

However, it is regrettable that too many parents insist on their children's instruction in matters that concern their future earthly destiny and neglect their children's religious education, which they regard as of little importance.

They take steps to get their child or children ready for First Communion, and that is all to the good. But children keep growing. Will their religious formation keep pace if no one helps them?

Teenagers may do well in secular studies yet remain on the level of a ten-year-old in religious education. Small wonder that some of them give up all practice of their religion.

Christian parents must understand that one of their principal duties is to provide for the religious education of their children. Normally they should do so by choosing a Catholic school even if the choice involves a monetary sacrifice. If cost puts a Catholic school out of reach for them, they then have the duty to supply the religious formation by other means.

Our American parishes have CCD programs where Catholic children and teenagers not in a parochial school are taught Catholic doctrine and practice.

In any event, our little ones should always receive at home their first Christian education.

It is the parents' duty to teach their children their first prayers and to speak to them about Jesus, about the Blessed Virgin, about the beautiful stories in the Gospels, and about the lives of the Saints. Parents should take them, when still very young, to the church to visit our Lord and explain to them what the statues, the pictures, and the Way of the Cross represent. This St. Rita's mother did.

It is also the duty of parents to instill in their little ones the meaning of sin (what turns us away from Jesus) and the meaning of the state of grace (Jesus present in our hearts).

Parents, moreover, should ensure that their children are prepared for their First Confession and their First Communion. Let them know that this Confession and this Communion are not optional practices but obligatory from the time a child is capable of making them.

Only a religious education of the kind described here can form true Catholic Christians.

PRAYER: TO ENSURE THE RELIGIOUS EDUCATION OF OUR CHILDREN

O St. Rita,
you had the great happiness
of being brought up by truly religious parents.
Raise up among us many parents like yours.
Let their principal care be
to lead their children to Jesus.
Let them be aware of their responsibility
and have all the understanding and all the tact
they need to fulfill their role.

Humbly ask the Holy Spirit
to help mothers be solicitous
for the faith and generosity of their children.

Let our little ones learn to be unselfish
and devoted to others.

Let our teenagers be resolved to do their best,
and let them be guided by a true love for Jesus.
May our Lord help them to remain
upright and pure in a world that is not.
The temptations they will face are so many and
    so great
that their perseverance will seem at times
to be compromised.

O Saint of most difficult cases,
help the parents of today
to educate the Catholics of tomorrow.
Amen.

FOURTH THURSDAY

Preparatory Prayer, 13

LIFE: A DREADED MARRIAGE THAT TURNS OUT WELL

R ITA wanted to be a nun. That seemed to be her vocation, inasmuch as she had always loved solitude and the life of prayer.

However, her aged parents wanted her to marry, perhaps because they had increasing need of her and desperately wished to keep her in the village.

Rita, ever docile, deferentially accepted what her parents called "a good match."

Certainly, her fiance, Paul Mancini, was not the ideal spouse. But possibly Rita's mildness could change his character for the better. After all, even someone who has been subject to a tormented youth can become a good father.

It was important that a girl have a home. At this period, marriages were made without consulting the young people involved and in accord with the interest of the parents. Rita consented, smiling in order to hide her tears.

Thus, at the age of eighteen Rita married Paul. The early years were very hard for her. Her husband was a loud and violent man who at times even hurt her. He is said to have been full of anger, vulgar, and debauched.

However, the latest research has unearthed data that tend to rehabilitate the man. He did not have all these vices, we are now told.

Yet it is no less true that the characters of the two spouses did not interact very well. For example, marital authority was manifested by the husband a little too harshly, frightening the timid Rita.

Moreover, Paul was a soldier in a troubled country, and his vocation was more important to him than his home. When he returned there battle-weary, he was often in a foul mood. Rita tried to compensate for this by her patience and her delicate nature.

Little by little, the two spouses drew closer together. Paul put forth efforts for the peace of the home, and the couple was relatively happy for fifteen years.

Under the influence of his bride, Paul became a good Christian. Rita's acceptance of the cross given her eventually brought conjugal happiness.

Therefore, it is with good reason that Catholics have made it a habit to entrust difficult matrimonial situations to St. Rita. She had experienced such situations and had succeeded in overcoming them by the only true victory: that of love that ends up being shared.

REFLECTION: EXAMPLE OF HEROIC PATIENCE

*S*OMETIMES *God's ways are incomprehensible. Rita seemed to have a call to the religious life, but Providence allowed her parents to direct her to the marriage state.*

This fact causes us to realize that God's plans are often much different from ours. He is far wiser than we are. He sees situations clearly in His Divine Wisdom, and we owe Him our trust.

Once God's will is clear, the only reasonable attitude is to submit to it. St. Rita did just that: she submitted to God's will.

We now understand, in the light of this Saint's experience, why God acted as He did. He wanted to give unhappy spouses a striking example of heroic patience.

So many men and women today are suffering the painful consequences of an ill-considered marriage. All too often these spouses, unlike Rita, have only themselves to blame. They chose to ignore the advice given them to think twice before getting married. Heeding only their passion, they rushed into a deplorable union.

When the time of illusions has passed, these spouses begin, too late, to comprehend the mistake they have made. Often they react with violence and ineptness. A struggle between two egotists ensues, and then they can think of no solution but the abomination of divorce. With that, their own two lives are shattered as well as those of their children who are always innocent victims.

People presume to say that they "must start over." Sometimes even parents who consider themselves devout Catholics give this shocking advice and encourage their son or daughter to enter into a new union outside the Church, which keeps them away from the Sacraments.

How much better to follow the example of Rita, the faithful wife. She endured difficult times, but her suffering was not in vain. She not only found the joy of a happy home but also saved her husband's soul. She was indeed a "peace-bearer" of Jesus Christ: "Blessed are the meek, for they shall inherit the land" (Matthew 5:4).

PRAYER: FOR THOSE
IN TROUBLED MARRIAGES

O St. Rita,
   make us understand
that a vocation is not only a matter of attraction.
Enable us to see clearly
that it is also a matter of finding,
in ordinary events,
God's will for us
and then accepting it

even if it seems to be baffling
and contrary to our wishes.

Teach those called to the marriage state
by the Lord
to reflect deeply on the delicate choice
that will influence their destiny.

Let them not be deceived by their feelings;
instead, let them look for the solid qualities
that keep a home united in the joy of the Lord.

Teach unhappy spouses the power
of patience and mildness.
Let them not give way to discouragement
but, like you, let them save
both the happiness of their home
and the soul of their spouse.
Amen.

FIFTH THURSDAY

Preparatory Prayer, p. 13

LIFE: HOME LIFE AND THE SERVICE OF OTHERS

THE little church in Roccaporena, where Rita was married, still stands today. Also in Roccaporena can still be seen the Mancini House, where Rita and her husband lived after the death of her parents. It is possible that the two couples lived there together.

Engaged couples from many countries like to have their promises blessed in the Mancini House, which has been made into a chapel. A precious relic of St. Rita, her blood-stained cloak, is kept in the chapel. Her wedding ring and her peasant rosary are kept in the convent in Cascia.

Rita's wedding ring represented at first the sacrifice she had to make. Her sadness, however, was changed to joy and blessings by the conversion of her husband. The rosary, like the blood-stained cloak, tells the secret of this conversion. Did not our Lord say that some categories of demons can only be driven out by prayer and penance?

Rita was always a praying soul. She had great devotion to the suffering Christ. Her rosary testifies to her devotion to Mary.

In the fifteenth century the method of the rosary was already well-known and widely used. People prayed the Hail Marys and meditated on the mysteries. The meditation is by far the main part.

We can easily imagine our Saint calling to mind the joys, the sorrows, and the glories of Jesus and Mary. We can picture her comparing events in her own life with the mysteries and drawing courage and hope from them.

Rita was not content with prayer alone. She lived at a time when bodily penances were much in favor. Sometimes they were practiced to excess, as in the confraternities of Flagellants.

Rita wore a hair shirt. She also would scourge herself, which accounts for the bloodstains on her cloak. To the official Lent she would add one and even two other "Lents" wherein she survived on only bread and water.

Not far from the Mancini House in Roccaporena there was a kind of small dispensary called the Lazaret. Here the sick poor were nursed by kindhearted women. Rita was among those nurses. Her historians speak of her increased generosity toward the poor. They add that "her husband approved."

REFLECTION: THE NEED FOR PENANCE

*A*LL *through her married life Rita was a model for the sincere Christian. What should be borne in mind, more than anything else, is her spirit of penance. This is more wor-*

thy of reflection than her meditative way of praying the rosary, or her heroic patience, or even her charity toward the poor.

In our day, people do not like to hear of penance. The Church herself has had to reduce our fast to almost nothing. Bodily mortification is seldom preached.

Present-day materialism has made the body king. Nothing is denied it; everything seems owed it. We seek comfort in all its forms. We seek it in defiance of all decency. We seek the pleasures of the senses, beginning with those of food and drink, on which so much is spent. A comparable sum, if not more, is spent to keep abreast of the latest fashions.

Crowning all is unbridled sensuality. "Your body is yours alone!" proclaims a pagan literature, relayed by immoral and degrading films. Not a few succumb to temptation, and many adults abandon all religious practice simply because, after their youth, Christian morality seems too hard for them to bear.

Against this deluge of pagan influence, almost no one dares to protest. Human respect paralyzes the people who should react and makes speechless the people who should speak out.

One person, and only one, has put forth a call to bring back the authentic Gospel; it is the Blessed Virgin. At Lourdes she repeated: "Penance, penance, penance!" At Fatima she let little Jacinta know that "sins of the flesh are the sins that lead the most souls to hell."

We who feel attracted to St. Rita should have the courage to examine the abyss that separates us from her spirituality in the matter of bodily penance. We should also ask her to help us practice some form of penance regularly.

PRAYER: TO FOSTER MORTIFICATION AND SACRIFICE

O St. Rita of Cascia,
you took the Gospel of penance seriously.
You knew how to master the instincts of your
  body
to keep it from oppressing your soul.
Help us,
have pity on us.

We too are swept up in the torrent of materialism.
Do not allow us to be lost in it,
nor any of the people we hold dear.
Give us a high regard for mortification,
seeing that it is indispensable.

In the present and the future
we have to defend ourselves
against the contagion of evil.
In the past
there is much we have to make amends for,
we who sometimes say we have never hurt
  anyone.

Yet the truth is
that by our sensuality we have hurt ourselves.

Shake off our torpor.
Help us to free ourselves.
Above all, teach us to protect our young
by instilling in them a love for God
and a desire for mortification and sacrifice.

These are the price of their purity,
and we know very well
that purity will be for them
the sole means of their perseverance in the
    faith:
"Blessed are the clean of heart,
for they shall see God" (Matthew 5:8).
Amen.

SIXTH THURSDAY

Preparatory Prayer, p. 13

LIFE: TWO SEVERE TRIALS—DEATHS OF PARENTS AND HUSBAND

RITA went through trials most people go through, particularly loss of dear ones in death. She was born of parents far along in years. Her life as a teenager was entirely devoted to them. She provided for their needs and made them happy when she agreed to get married.

It is probable that Rita and her husband lived with her parents at the Mancini House. Living together inevitably causes some problems that cannot be avoided. However, the frightful temperament of her husband made the situation even more troublesome. Rita had to be an angel of meekness to keep the house at peace and the parents comfortable in their home. This situation lasted for three years, precisely the period in which she was "the patient wife."

Antonio and Amy Lotti seem to have died a few days apart—he on March 19, feast of St. Joseph; and she on March 25, feast of the Annunciation. To us, going to heaven together looks like a touching blessing of Christian love.

It is beautiful to see a husband and wife who, to an advanced age, stood by each other for better or for worse. It is also beautiful to see them blessed with going to the grave in close succession.

Rita missed her parents. She was cheered, however, by the change in her husband around the time of their death.

After the change there were fifteen years of marital bliss. Then, one evening, came the shocking news: returning from Cascia, Paul was assassinated. This tragedy remains enigmatic. For fifteen years this man, formerly so cruel and fearsome to the neighbors, had given no one any reason to hate him. No doubt, he was the victim of a vendetta.

Paul's assassination was an agony for his poor wife. To the shattering loss of her human happiness was added a gnawing anxiety over her husband's soul. She knew that a sudden death is always a dreadful thing. The year was probably 1417.

REFLECTION: THE DANGER OF SUDDEN DEATH

*H*ER *parents and husband were among the people Rita loved most here on earth. When she lost them to death, each loss was a severe affliction, alleviated however by Christian hope.*

Rita had faith ardent enough and logical enough to repeat what St. Augustine wrote after the death of his mother, St. Monica: "We must not mourn too much for our mother, because she did not die unhappy. She is not even dead in the least. We are convinced of that."

We can imagine the veneration Rita must have had for her deceased parents. They became the heavenly protectors of her home. Often she spoke of them to her children, and often she took the children to the grave of their grandparents as though on a pilgrimage to the grave of Saints.

At prayer in common (meals, mornings, evenings) she undoubtedly invoked her parents, and at Masses that she asked to be offered in their honor the whole family was present. She offered them "in their honor" provisionally: on condition that such prayers might still be needed for the repose of their souls.

The death of her husband staggered Rita even more because it was a sudden death. Today, our faith is so weak that we could easily be led to envy people dying suddenly. "At least they didn't suffer," we hear it said.

Some people are senseless enough to think that a sudden death is not a calamity. Yet nothing is quite so dangerous as to appear before the Lord without having had time to think about it, to prepare for it, to be sorry for sins and receive forgiveness.

Hence, the Church in the Litany of the Saints puts on our lips this insistent supplication: "From sudden death, deliver us, O Lord."

PRAYER: TO OBTAIN THE CHRISTIAN MEANING OF DEATH

O St. Rita,
you had your kind heart pained
by your various periods of mourning.
Obtain for us an understanding of the Christian
    meaning of death.
So easily we let ourselves mourn
like people who have no hope.

Very often we think first of ourselves,
of our great sorrow,
sometimes even of the material difficulties
that follow the death of our dear ones.

We should, instead, think first of them
and their new situation on the threshold of
    Eternal Life,
which is so mysterious for us.

We have been instructed in the faith
and we know that God's judgment
in regard to our dear ones
has already been carried out.
If our dead are in purgatory,
we know we can help them get released
and entered in the "place of refreshment, light,
    and peace"
(mentioned in the Eucharistic Prayer at Mass).

Remind us, then, O St. Rita,
that in this respect one thing alone matters:
that we avail ourselves of all the means

that God in His mercy has given us
to bring about their deliverance.

Remind us that we can offer our poor merits
together with the infinite merits of the Lord
and have the Holy Sacrifice of the Mass offered
    for them.

The Eucharistic Christ then serves
as the living hyphen between us and our dear
    ones.
With Him, in Him, and through Him
we remain united with the ones we call our
    dead
but who are more alive than we.
The certainty of meeting again in eternity
then possesses our hearts.

We have the feeling that families here on earth
are destined to be brought together again in
    heaven.
Humanly speaking, that is the greatest consola-
    tion.

Help us,
O St. Rita,
to attain this as fully as possible,
in Christ our Lord.
Amen.

SEVENTH THURSDAY

Preparatory Prayer, p. 13.

LIFE: A CHRISTIAN MOTHER

RITA had two children, two sons. There was very little age difference; perhaps they were even twins. They must have been born in the early years of the marriage, since they were already young men when their father died and Rita had been married for only eighteen years.

Tradition is not entirely in agreement as to their names. Apparently, one was called John-James and the other Paul-Mary. Rita was a young mother with a lot of good sense. It never occurred to her to give the children a non-religious name that may have been in style.

In this matter of names, Rita's times were less frivolous than ours. When choosing a name for their children, people thought especially of giving them a Patron Saint who could be an example to them on earth and an intercessor in heaven.

Concerning her sons' education, we only know that in their early childhood Rita used to take them to the "Lazaret" to visit the poor and the infirm. Each visit was a real lesson in charity. Rita's way of teaching the lesson is much better than simply teaching from a book.

The father approved of this method of education and helped his wife as much as he could. When he felt a surge of anger, he would leave the house so as not to scandalize the children. This should be recognized as important, since care must be taken lest the young perceive some hostility between their parents.

After their father's assassination, one lesson Rita could not get across to her grown sons was the lesson of forgiveness. She herself had made the heroic act of forgiving the murderers with all her heart. After this merciful step and because of it, people said God made known to her that her husband's soul was saved.

Instilling in her sons the same sentiments of mercy and forgiveness proved impossible. The sons were much like their contentious ancestors and had grown up in a time of hatred. They were also carried away by their false sense of honor under the guise of a "vendetta."

When Rita reminded them of the Lord's teaching: "Love your enemies. . . . Pray for those who persecute you" (Matthew 6:44), she felt she was not understood, much less followed. She was afraid her sons might lose their souls by believing they were honoring their father's memory.

Therefore, in an act of heroism, Rita formulated a prayer that was in keeping with her Christian sentiments but crushed her mother's heart. Indeed, she uttered those stupefying words: "Take them, my God, rather than they offend You."

The prayer was heard; for a chronicler wrote that Rita's two sons "were called to a better life." God took them home, and they died the Christian way after renouncing their hatred and ill-will.

For the Saint of the Impossible, here was her first hopeless case. It turned out very well indeed.

REFLECTION: FORGIVENESS OF OTHERS

*O*NE *of the most difficult forms of charity is to forgive offenses. We have all suffered offenses. There is little comparison, however, between what we have had to bear and what was weighing on St. Rita's heart after her husband's assassination.*

She remembered Jesus on the Cross interceding for His executioners: "Father, forgive them, for they know not what they do" (Luke 23:24). Perhaps we do not have love enough to model ourselves on our Divine Lord and to react as He did.

Let us at least have intelligence enough to know where our interest lies. Our Lord said and repeated in the Gospel that He would deal with us the same way we had dealt with our neighbor.

If we want to be forgiven, then let us begin by forgiving others. As the Apostle St. James wrote in his Epistle (2:13): "Judgment is without mercy to those who have not shown mercy; but mercy triumphs over judgment."

We ought to reflect more on St. Rita's prayer regarding her sons: "Take them, rather than they offend You." This was nearly like the prayer of a queen of France, though she was not a Saint: "My son, you know how much I love you," said Blanche of Castille to the young Louis IX, "and yet I would rather see you dead at my feet than guilty of a single mortal sin."

What a lesson for us and how praiseworthy it would be if, like these truly Christian mothers (Rita and Queen Blanche), we thought much more about the soul of our children than about the health of their body.

PRAYER: TO PRACTICE TRUE CHARITY

O St. Rita,
raise up in our families
mothers who are truly educators.
So many mothers around us
only think about their children's physical life.
Others, it is true, also concern themselves
with the intellectual development of their children.
Few mothers, however, do "the one thing necessary,"
which is to guide their children
to encounter the Lord.

Obtain for us, O St. Rita,
what is sorely needed:
many more mothers who think first
about helping their children live in the state of grace
and about instilling in them Godlike charity.

PRAYER WITH ST. RITA

L ORD,
You gave St. Rita the grace to love her enemies.
By her merits and intercession,
enable us to forgive those who have injured us
and so to merit the reward promised to the
meek and the mournful.

Grant, O my God,
that by the intercession of our Saint,
we too may carry in our hearts the marks of
Your charity
and constantly enjoy the benefits of lasting
peace.
Amen.

EIGHTH THURSDAY

Preparatory Prayer, p. 13

LIFE: KNOCKING AT THE CONVENT DOOR

THE year 1417 was a sorrowful one for Rita. In the course of it she lost her husband and both her sons. For the Church, it was a hopeful year, bringing the end of the Great Schism.

Rita was thirty-six; Joan of Arc was five. Rita seemed to be all alone in the world. As a matter of fact she was not alone. She was living with her "dead," those who had returned to the Father and had become her personal Saints. She talked to them, prayed to them, and asked them for advice.

Rita probably had a kind of homesickness for the religious life. She had always lived in accord with the spirit of this kind of life. Poverty, chastity, and obedience are its pillars. In her years as a married woman she had tried to practice them as much as possible.

She was obedient to her aged parents despite the difficulty sometimes encountered in keeping old people content. She was obedient to her husband, even in the abusive years.

She practiced poverty, not from avarice or fear of being in want but from a desire to give more alms.

She practiced chastity in its conjugal form, a type often more difficult than the chastity of the unmarried, which is respected by so few Christians today.

Good as it was, for Rita life outside the convent was not sufficient. She wanted to make a more complete gift of herself. The convent of Augustinian nuns in Cascia attracted her. When she applied for admission, the convent, named after St. Mary Magdalene, turned her down.

The rejection had nothing to do with Rita's being a widow. In the Church widows always have been a particularly cherished and assisted class.

Something quite different was at work. In the convent in Cascia there were nuns who belonged to the clan that was hostile to the clan to which Rita belonged.

Rita would have to bring about a reconciliation between the two parties. Only then could she enter the convent without bringing along an element of division.

This seemed to be a superhuman enterprise. On the human level her case did appear to be impossible.

The solution? It seemed to come from heaven. Rita had her advocates—St. John the Baptist, St. Augustine, and St. Nicholas of Tolentine, who had inspired her vocation.

By their help and intercession Rita overcame a seemingly impossible obstacle: the hatred that separated many families of Cascia and that had already caused the death of her husband. The spiral of vendettas had to be stopped.

In order to put an end to these feelings of wrath and acts of vengeance, the widow became a messenger of peace. With humility and courage, she went from house to house, asking all the families who were at odds to be reconciled with one another.

At the same time, she besought the Lord through the intermediary of her "Saint Advocates." And God granted her this miracle of peace—for herself and for her village.

Rita willed that this act of reconciliation should be committed to writing and signed before a notary in accord with custom. And then, with the signed agreement in hand, she was finally able to pass through the formerly inaccessible convent of St. Mary Magdalene. Such is the historical fact.

However, this fact has been transformed into a legendary event by the popular imagination. It has become a kind of "flight" of Rita—accompanied by St. John the Baptist, St. Augustine, and St. Nicholas of Tolentine—from the crag of Roccaporena to the cloister of the convent.

Her heavenly "patrons" had presumably accomplished her entry despite all doors being shut, and the religious community could no longer refuse to give consent!

REFLECTION: BE RECONCILED WITH
ONE ANOTHER

N*OTHING is impossible to those who work for reconciliation. From her parents, Rita had come to understand and admire the role of messengers of peace and good relations. Peace is the subject of one of the Beatitudes pronounced by Christ: "Blessed are peacemakers, for they shall be called children of God" (Matthew 5:9).*

Like a butterfly, she lightly ascended and descended countless stairways, both outside and inside homes, from the center of Cascia to the most distant villages. She asked everyone in them to be reconciled with her, a condition that she knew was indispensable before consecrating herself to God.

Such reconciliation is even more important than any kind of sacrifice according to the words of our Lord Himself: "When you present your offering at the altar and remember that your brother has something against you, leave your gift at the altar and go and be reconciled with him" (Matthew 5:23-24).

Therefore, we must be reconciled with our brothers in order to be truly united with God. Then only will we be able to offer Him our praise as well as our prayers and requests. And the Lord will in turn grant us His grace.

Following St. Rita's example, let us be reconciled with one another: spouses with each

*other; children among themselves and with
their parents, friends and neighbors with one
another. The peace in the world that we so
desire can only come when there is peace in our
personal and social lives.*

PRAYER: TO OBTAIN THE GIFT OF RECONCILIATION

O my God,
grant me the gift of reconciliation
with members of my family
and with others.

May I take the time to listen to everyone
who has no one with whom to speak.
May I listen willingly to all
who cannot express themselves,
or who do not dare to do so,
thus giving them the opportunity to be heard.

I could never hope
to listen to everyone,
but I can adopt an attitude of listening
toward everyone with whom I come into contact.

When I strive to listen to my neighbors,
I do for them
what You, my God, have done for me.

By Your grace,
make me a messenger of reconciliation.
Amen.

NINTH THURSDAY
Preparatory Prayer, p. 13
LIFE: THE MIRACLE OF THE VINE

WITH God's help, Rita entered the convent of St. Mary Magdalene in Cascia. She was forty years old and already had a remarkable life as wife and mother behind her. Just the same, she had to make her novitiate.

For people with a strong personality the novitiate can be a trying time. Superiors tend to test them by forming them in the virtues of humility and obedience.

What is called "the miracle of the vine" may have happened during Rita's novitiate. It is inspired by an old story found in an ancient book, John Cassian's *Conferences*. Cassian founded the monastery of St. Victor in Marseilles at the beginning of the fifth century, about a thousand years before St. Rita.

According to the *Conferences*, a superior wanted to test the obedience of one of his monks. He told him to water, every day, a dead branch stuck into the ground. The branch never flowered, so the superior threw it away and effectively ended the test.

Mother Abbess of Cascia did something similar, though the ending was not the same. She told Rita to water daily, over a long period of time, a dry wooden stick she had asked her to bring into the yard and plant next to a wall.

Rita obeyed scrupulously. She watered the wooden stick every day, even when rain was falling. She kept up the daily watering for as long as the imposed obedience required it.

Tradition says that one day this wooden stick began to bud, then to flower miraculously. It became a vine that produced grapes of a form and taste unknown anywhere else.

Tradition also says that the people soon began to bring some of these grapes to the Holy Father and to Cardinals and distinguished benefactors of the Augustinian Order.

At the present time, grapes produced by the "Vine of the Miracle" are blessed and given to benefactors of the convent in Cascia.

This tradition is beautiful and filled with instruction for us. It teaches that absolute obedience based on the love for God will never lack for recompense. No matter what the circumstances may be, it will make us better persons.

After completing her novitiate Rita was allowed to make her profession. She took the vows of poverty, chastity, and obedience. By these vows she made a threefold solemn promise to God.

The following night she had a dream in which she saw a ladder. Its top reached to heaven; leaning against it was her beloved Lord. The ladder recalls the ladder of Jacob, which the Patriarch saw in a vision when an exchange of promises, a Covenant, was struck between God and himself.

Like Jacob, Rita found a message in the ladder. As one of her earliest biographers notes, it was a very clear sign to her that by the steps of the three solemn vows she would reach the summit of Christian perfection.

REFLECTION: POVERTY, CHASTITY, AND OBEDIENCE

WE also, Christians living in the world, should strive to make our life an ascent. We, of course, do not have the obligation to practice poverty, chastity, and obedience in the same way as men and women religious. These basic virtues are nonetheless necessary for us also, beginning with obedience.

Let us not forget that our Lord redeemed the world by obedience.

Reparation for something is made by its contrary. Against the cold of winter we try to create some warmth, for example. The same goes for reparation for sin. Sin is essentially disobedience. Reparation for it is made by the most perfect obedience possible.

That is why "Christ became obedient unto death" (Philippians 2:8). Combining our obedience with His remains for us the best way to take part in His Redemption of all the ones we love. Let us, then, be obedient to God as perfectly as possible.

Let us bear in mind that Christ makes His will known to us by His Commandments, by His Gospel, by the teachings of His Church, and even by our fellow citizens. He also makes it known by the events of our life, be they trials or happy occasions. Whether this Divine will is agreeable to us or seems painful, let us learn to accept it joyously.

Like St. Rita watering the wooden stick, let us not discuss, let us not analyze. Let us simply obey with eyes closed and heart wide open.

Let us also have the spirit of poverty and not be greedy for gain. Let us remember how insistently the Lord and His Gospel warn us about the love of money. To get more and more of it some Christians do not hesitate to transgress God's Law. In its quest they come to regard Sunday work as altogether normal.

Little by little the conscience of such people is corrupted. To them the demands of the most elementary justice are no longer so evident. They make shady business deals and take advantage of the ignorance or misery of others. But because of their corrupted conscience they make light of such transgressions and never dream of mentioning them in the Sacrament of Reconciliation.

What of the duty to practice the most elementary charity, e.g., to give alms? We may not like it, but it does require us to give from our abundance to people lacking the necessities.

Nonetheless, when someone begs alms from people who consider themselves devout, it often happens that what they give is ridiculously meager. Yet our Lord said that we will be judged on our charity toward others.

PRAYER: TO PRACTICE THE EVANGELICAL VIRTUES

O St. Rita,
you carried out faithfully
the Gospel of Jesus Christ.
Put in our hearts the conviction
that the Christian life is not just a question of
    devotion
but rather consists in doing God's will in every-
    thing:
"Not everyone who says to Me: 'Lord, Lord,'
will enter the Kingdom of heaven,
but only the person who does My Father's will"
    (Matthew 7:21).

Jesus also said:
"If you love Me,
keep My Commandments" (Matthew 14:15).

Help us, then, O St. Rita,
to set aside our own will
and to seek what God wants,
in chastity, which is at times difficult to
    observe,
as well as in justice and in charity.

When you see us attached to things of the
    world,
for example, to money,
help us to free ourselves.

Make us generous in giving to others,
in coming to the aid of people in need,
of the elderly in particular,
and of the truly poor,
who are always the most undemanding.

May our charity not be in words alone
but also in deeds.

Teach us to deprive ourselves occasionally
so as to have more to give
and thus,
like you,
to be true disciples of the Lord Jesus.
Amen.

TENTH THURSDAY

Preparatory Prayer, p. 13

LIFE: THE STIGMATA OF THE CROWN OF THORNS

IT is hard for us to imagine how much the Cross was venerated in medieval times. This veneration was partly an outgrowth of the Crusades.

In the thirteenth century devotion to the Crucifix was so ingrained in St. Francis of Assisi that he received the Stigmata on his own body. This happened at Alverno, not far from Cascia.

The following century St. Catherine of Siena received the same favor as Francis, but our Lord let her keep the pain of her Stigmata without making the Stigmata themselves visible to others.

As for Rita, she too was favored with a mystical phenomenon fifteen years before her death. On Good Friday of the year 1442, she went with her Sisters, as was the custom, to the parish church for the Office of the Passion of our Lord.

The ardent and moving preaching of the Friar entrusted with the Lenten exercises touched Sister Rita so much that she was spiritually overwhelmed.

Returning to the convent in haste, she ran to kneel before a fourteenth-century fresco that was in a little chapel, a decrepit oratory next to the choir stalls of the Sisters.

The fresco, which pictures a crucifix, still exists.

A biographer notes: "Rita began to ask Christ most ardently to make her feel at least one of the many thorns that had pierced His brow.

"What she asked for, she received. She felt the desired hurt. But also, and from then on, she was afflicted by an incurable wound that would remain with her till death.

"The wound was a true Stigmata, not just a scar. It was an open wound, purulent and fetid, that inflicted terrible suffering on Rita.

"The wound resisted all attempts at healing, and it never left her during the last fifteen years of her life—except during her pilgrimage to Rome."

Those who go to Cascia on pilgrimage are moved upon visiting the chapel of the miraculous Christ, also known as the "Hermitage of the Thorn," as well as Rita's little cell. They are the two historical places in which people sense the presence of faith.

In her little chapel Rita created what she called "stations" of the Passion of our Lord. In her cell she made one part a representation of Calvary, another of the Sepulcher, and so on.

Rita prayed continually before these stations, which were her "way of the cross." Many times the physical impressions made on her by the stations were so intense that she fell into a swoon.

REFLECTION: FOCUSING ON
CHRIST'S PASSION

IF we compare our reaction to Christ's sufferings with the profound reactions of the Saints, we may find that the Saints put us to shame. They are deeply moved by His sufferings. We seem to be coldly indifferent.

As it is with so many other realities of our Faith, so it is with the sorrowful Passion: we do not give it enough thought.

For example, few Christians today still pray the Way of the Cross. It is, nevertheless, a salutary devotion. It teaches the gravity of sin by reminding us of what it took to atone for sin.

Perhaps a short meditation on the scourged Christ would make us ashamed of all the sins we commit by indulging our bodies. Or a short meditation on the crown of thorns could make us less self-centered, less conceited in the presence of God made Man. He wanted no other signs of His Kingship on earth than this humiliating and painful emblem, together with derision and outrages.

If we thought of Christ more often as carrying His Cross, we would probably get a better understanding of what a human life is all about. We would find that for the most part it consists in carrying a cross.

Under the weight of this cross we fall again and again, despite the comforters encountered along the way: the Virgin Mother, Simon of Cyrene. the friendly Veronica.

What Jesus taught the women of Jerusalem He would teach us. He would say it does no good to lament. He would say we must move into action, must deprive ourselves, must be one with His Cross as the living Crucifix of Calvary.

Then, crowning His teaching, He would say we must accept the entire will of the Father to the very end, to the very last word: "It is finished."

Instead of all that, we keep looking for some sort of easy religion, one that does not affect us too much. A little devotion to this or that Saint dispenses us, we tell ourselves, from all the rest.

We have lost the sense of sin and the punishments it deserves. This is the reason our contrition is so often insufficient. Our mentality has drifted away from the Faith without our becoming aware of it; we have evolved into a society of Christians without Christianity.

Putting ourselves in the presence of the stigmatic and enthusiastic follower of Christ that Rita was, let us pray as follows.

PRAYER: TO OBTAIN TRUE CONTRITION

BECAUSE of St. Rita's merits we beseech
You,
O Lord,
to pierce our hearts
with the thorn of supernatural sorrow
that consists in true contrition.
Free us from all our sins by Your grace,
so that we may offer You the Eucharist
with clean hearts and a new spirit.

And each time we have been nourished
and made stronger by Holy Communion,
engrave on our mentality
the Stigmata of Christ's Love and His Passion
so that we may remain always
in Your Peace.
We ask You this, O Blessed Trinity,
through Jesus Christ our Lord.
Amen.

ELEVENTH THURSDAY

Preparatory Prayer, p. 13

LIFE: THE ROMAN JUBILEE

JUBILEES have existed since the year 1300. They used to be proclaimed every fifty years; now they occur every twenty-five years.

In former times jubilees were the occasion for making a penitential pilgrimage to Rome. They came to a close with the great joy of a plenary indulgence, the most formal and most generous of all.

The jubilee of 1450 was particularly important. The Church had regained her unity and her internal peace only three years earlier.

The regaining of this peace and unity came after the disorders caused by the Council of Basle and then by the Duke of Savoy, Amadeus VIII, who had agreed to become the antipope Felix V.

More than ever, Rome was seen as the center of restored unity. People came to Rome from everywhere.

These pilgrimages of former times required far greater physical endurance than those of today. People had to go on foot. They had to ford rivers, brave the elements, and sleep out in the open. Yet the crowds were overflowing.

Monasteries and convents opened their doors to let men and women religious gain their jubilee indulgence. Rita also wanted to go to Rome, but because of her fetid wound it seemed out of the question.

Mother Abbess of Cascia did not risk much when she told Rita she could go as soon as she was cured. This good Superior was ill-prepared to deal with the woman who some day would become the "Saint of the Impossible."

Rita prayed and the wound dried up. So she could go, after all. A small group of Augustinian Sisters from Cascia, with Rita at the head, went across the Apennines, through Rieti, and over the via Flaminia. It was a picturesque route, but a long and difficult one.

On the way the Sisters began to wonder if they had enough money to carry their pilgrimage to the end. This preoccupation struck our Saint as not at all evangelical. She carried the purse, and no one took offense when she threw it disdainfully in a stream the little group was crossing.

"Think, my Sisters," she said, "what deception the world would have about us if it saw us provided with money. If, however, we disdain wealth and truly show ourselves to be Sisters of poverty, all will know that we are true Religious in the spirit of Christ."

To us, throwing the purse in the stream may seem to have been improper or foolhardy. No, it was simply the reaction of a soul having an abhorrence of money, for love of which people will commit so many sins.

The group made it to Rome. The marvelous Basilica of St. Peter as we know it today did not yet exist. In the old Constantinian Church the pilgrims went to venerate the remains of the Holy Apostles. They also visited the Roman Colosseum, where so many martyrs had been the prey of wild beasts.

In the Church of the Holy Cross of Jerusalem, they prayed before relics of the Passion. For Rita who had received the Stigmata of the thorn, what an emotional experience it must have been to see there, devoutly preserved, two thorns from the painful crown.

Above all, the pilgrims saw the Pope, "the gentle Christ on earth," as St. Catherine of Siena had said not long before. In him is embodied the mystery of the Church, ever One and ever Holy despite the weaknesses of the people that make it up.

The Roman pilgrimage was certainly a high point in Rita's life, but in the fuller view of this humble Sister there were other high points, less known or even unsuspected.

For who would have thought that Rita would be one of the best workers in the renewal of the Roman Church? Above all, who could have foreseen that this dear woman, old before her time, emaciated and lost in the crowd, would, four hundred and fifty years later, be solemnly canonized in the new Basilica of Michelangelo?

REFLECTION: THE VALUE OF PILGRIMAGES

PEOPLE have always had a liking for pilgrimages. They have felt that there are "places where the Spirit breathes," places on our earth where the spiritual seems to assert itself more than anywhere else.

Sometimes they are places to which heaven has inclined in famous apparitions, as at Lourdes or Fatima. They are also the many places where Saints have lived, from which they took their flight to the Father's house, and where their bodies await the signal of the definitive resurrection.

Crowds are attracted to these privileged places as if to escape the daily routine. The journey to these places of pilgrimage takes the act of denial of self out of the abstract and brings it into the concrete. The journey does the same for purification of the soul and for the effort to gain more enlightenment.

The fact is that people always return spiritually strengthened from a pilgrimage properly made. The key to such a pilgrimage consists in going not as mere tourists attentive to their own comfort, nor as idle curiosity-seekers, and especially not as snobs contemptuous of their "inferiors."

To be fruitful a pilgrimage requires preparation of the soul—in particular, its purification or

*cleansing. There is no use going to Rome, to
Cascia, or to any other holy place without being
in the state of grace and without wanting to benefit so as to lead a more Christian life.*

PRAYER: TO FIX OUR EYES ON HEAVEN DURING OUR EARTHLY PILGRIMAGE

O St. Rita,
  you are the model for our devotion
when we want to undertake a pilgrimage.
Help us to benefit always,
as you yourself did,
from the graces
that this ancient Christian tradition may bring
    to us.

Keep us friendly and cheerful on the way
but not too concerned with our comfort.
Make us see
that the journey to any house of God on earth
is a symbol of another journey,
in which neither the effort
nor the self-denial should be feared,
because at its end lies the City of God.

We are such awful stay-at-homes,
so comfortably settled in our trivial, mediocre
    lives.
Obtain for us the will and the courage
to make the journey to new horizons
and bring our brothers and sisters along.

In addition, enable us to have
a right understanding of money
so that we may make use of it
without becoming overly attached to it.

Obtain for us—
to crown all our efforts—
the will to go ever farther, ever higher,
toward the Light of God!
Amen.

TWELFTH THURSDAY
Preparatory Prayer, p. 13

LIFE: DAYS AS A RECLUSE

MADE in a Christian way, a pilgrimage is a source of enriching grace. It is a time filled with religious activity, but that time soon comes to an end. People then have to resume a normal life.

The main thing is to live that normal life with more heart than before. This is precisely what Rita did.

Returning from Rome, she went back to her convent in Cascia. There she lived the last years of her earthly sojourn and became ever more spiritual.

Rita was scarcely back home when the wound on her forehead opened again. This was an indication from Providence that she was being called to resume her life as a recluse. In her secluded cell she seemed more than ever a stranger to the world and even to the other Sisters.

For a recluse such as Rita, the contemplative life appeared to be all that mattered. She allotted all her time to prayer. A biographer remarks that she could not seem to refrain from praying. She consecrated her nights to prayer and, with the coming of dawn, bemoaned the interruption of the heavenly conversations.

Completely spiritualized, she was impervious to the material life. She lived on the Holy Eucharist, which she received often—at a time when daily Communion was not yet an established custom.

The case of Rita is similar to that of some contemporary mystics. In both there is a strange parallel as regards material things. Just as some people only live for the flesh and the senses and finish by becoming totally materialized, so souls completely lost in God end up, in some sense, by spiritualizing even their body.

The fame of this recluse began to spread. People came in streams to recommend themselves to her. They came to see her even from distant lands. So great was the attraction that the convent became a center of pilgrimage.

Even during her lifetime Rita obtained miracles. For example, a woman came to recommend to her a gravely ill daughter and on returning home found that daughter restored to health. In moments like this, Rita's physical sufferings became more acute by a mysterious Communion of Saints and interchanging of merits.

Because, in spite of herself, she attracted so many people, what Jesus once said of Himself is applicable to Rita: "When I am lifted up from earth [when I am crucified], I will draw all to Myself" (John 12:32). And on another occasion: "If anyone believes in Me, rivers of living water will flow from him" (John 7:38).

REFLECTION: THE CONTRIBUTION OF
CONTEMPLATIVES

W*E do not believe enough in this influence of mystic souls. We tend to attach value only to what is visibly useful. We understand, for example, the dedication of hospital Sisters. The contemplative life we find hard to understand.*

It seems normal to us that God has called men and women to make Him known and loved, for example, parish priests and missionaries.

On the other hand, we have little understanding of persons who do not feel themselves called to the direct apostolate yet leave the world to pursue a life of prayer. These are the contemplatives, who add some manual work to their life to support themselves and do good around them.

Such people are called by God to the contemplative life. That call is made known by an attraction to this kind of life and an aptitude for it.

The collective influence exercised by men and women religious is a positive force. Only those who never have had anything to do with a convent or monastery can be ignorant of this.

In our materialistic world, abbeys and convents are like oases where spiritual things thrive. People drained by the secular life go there to regain their lost energy. Some great nations, for example, England, were evange-

lized solely by monasteries planted on their soil when they did not yet know Jesus.

Today, a serious retreat of some day's duration in a monastery or convent is one of the best means of change for people who are Christian by habit alone and feel that true Christianity has to be something other than what they are practicing.

Our life needs to be directed more toward God. To make this happen there is nothing like living awhile in the surroundings of a community of men or women who have understood that the "one thing necessary" is to know God and live increasingly in union with Him and in intense charity with their brothers and sisters.

PRAYER: TO DISCOVER WHAT GOD EXPECTS OF US

O St. Rita,
  on this earth you never exercised the true apostolate
so much as when you were a recluse.
Make us understand
that the Lord does not want our works
as much as He wants our love.

Enable us to see
that what gives value to our life
is not this or that form of the apostolate
but our conformity to the Father's will.
Help us, then,
to find out what the Father expects of each of
  us.

May we follow our vocation
not because we want to satisfy our fancy
but because it is primarily the expression of the
    Divine will.
May we not fall into illusion
but know how to distinguish between our pos-
    sibilities
and our true aptitudes.

Obtain for us, O St. Rita,
the grace to see clearly
and to make use of the gift of counsel
from our Confirmation,
so that always and everywhere
we may give our life
the maximum of fruitfulness.

We know we will succeed in this
if in all things we seek to know
the Father's will
and conform to it.
Help us in our quest to do so.
Amen.

THIRTEENTH THURSDAY
Preparatory Prayer, p. 13

LIFE: FINAL MIRACLES—ROSES AND FIGS

AFTER her Roman pilgrimage, as we have seen, Rita lived as a recluse during which she became increasingly spiritualized. She suffered much, but she bore her suffering with good cheer.

Nevertheless, it is idle now to look for her in the fasts and mortifications that marked the prime of her life but had become things of the past because of her physical condition. She was an elderly woman filled with pains and could only accept the trials that flowed therefrom.

Rita understood "good suffering," the kind by which the Christian shares in the redemptive work of Christ. Like St. Paul, she could say: "I rejoice in the sufferings I endure for you. In my own flesh I fill up what is still lacking in regard to the sufferings of Christ, for the sake of His Body, the Church" (Colossians 1:24).

Her last winter was one of those hard seasons encountered in Cascia, which sometimes is cut off from the rest of the world by huge accumulations of snow.

A cousin, a gracious woman, came to see Rita and asked: "What can I do for you?" She replied: "I would like a rose from my little garden." The cousin thought Rita was delirious.

The cousin went back to Roccaporena and had forgotten the request when, by chance, she was walking near the former garden of St. Rita. And there, in the garden, was a bright red rose on one of the rosebushes. The cousin took it and brought it to the ailing Rita.

Today a bronze sculpture commemorates the event and, each year on May 22, roses are blessed before being brought to the sick, just as the cousin brought Rita the rose from the miraculous rosebush.

A cutting from the rosebush was planted in the garden of the convent in Cascia. For five hundred years, nothing has been able to cause the cutting to die. It has actually grown into an enormous bush of whitish and lovely scented roses.

When the cousin brought the beautiful rose, Rita said to her: "Since you have been so kind as to bring me the rose, I would like you now to bring me two fresh figs from the fig tree in my garden." Though it was not the time for figs, the fig tree had produced its fruit. Once again a miracle came about. Is not Rita truly "the Saint of the Impossible"?

REFLECTION: THE NEED TO PRODUCE WORTHY FRUITS OF CHARITY

*T*HIS anecdote about the figs contrasts with the Lord's parable about the barren fig tree:

"A man had a fig tree planted in his vineyard, and he came out looking for fruit on it but did not find any. He said to the vinedresser, 'Behold, for three years now I have come looking for fruit on this fig tree and found none. Cut it down. Why should it clutter up the ground?' " (Luke 13:6-7).

Too often we are much like this fig tree. We produce so little fruit. We give the impression of being on earth only for the purpose of seeking our petty personal comfort. It was not like this for St. Rita, whose life was so rich in the eyes of God.

Let us be convinced that we have already lost too much time. Sometimes, of course, we have put ourselves to work. Perhaps we have even worked hard, but it was for selfish ends, for ourselves or our kindred. It was not for God or our neighbor. The time has come to think a little more about others and produce worthy fruits of charity.

One of the kindest works of mercy is to visit people who are suffering, the sick, the aged, the lonely, and open to them our heart and, when necessary, our purse. Let us bring them the blessed roses of St. Rita, but let us also bring them our encompassing understanding.

May we really be charitable; that will be the best way to show that we are truly Christian. Let us not forget that often a visit to a suffering person is more pleasing to God than lengthy prayers.

PRAYER: TO SEE CHRIST IN OTHERS

O St. Rita,
you made such good use of your life.
Help us not to be barren fig trees.
Make us understand the Divine words of the
Gospel:
"What does it profit anyone
to gain the whole world
and suffer the loss of one's soul?"
(Matthew 16:26).
"Lay up a treasure that will not fail you in
heaven,
where no thief comes near
nor any moth destroys"
(Luke 12:33).
Make us understand that we lay up this treasure
mostly through goodness to others,
through patience and alms.

All your life,
O St. Rita,
you were at the service of the sick and the
aged.
Help us to imitate you.
Give us the will to visit people who are lonely
and people who are suffering.
May our approach to them
be a source of comfort and joy.

Gladden our heart so that we may find,
when we are near these people,
the words that fit,

the words that console and elevate them to
   God.
May we also deprive ourselves now and then
so as to bring people who lack the necessities
the help of our alms.

Make us see the Lord in all the poor and needy,
and make us have for them
the same respect and love we would have
in the presence of the very Person of Jesus
   Christ.
Change our hearts,
which are still too hard;
warm them by contact with the fire of Christian
   charity.

By loving our brothers and sisters in truth and
   in practice,
may we come to join in the heavenly Kingdom
those who, like yourself,
practiced goodness and charity on earth.
Amen.

FOURTEENTH THURSDAY

Preparatory Prayer, p. 13

LIFE: THE TRUE DAY OF BIRTH

FOR us, Christians with a vision overly focused on this world, death is the great expiration, painful and often dreaded. For Saints, it is the day of their birth in heaven and, later, the day of their feast, when the Christian community joyfully sings their praises.

May 22 is a date dear to all friends of St. Rita because on that date, in the year 1457, she took her flight to heaven. Some biographers say that three days earlier our Lord appeared to her in the company of the Blessed Virgin. Questions crossed her mind:

"When, Jesus, can I possess You forever? When can I come into Your presence?"

"Soon, but not yet."

"Well, when?"

"In three days you will be with Me in heaven."

The assurance brought great joy to Rita. The waiting was about to be over, and she felt serene.

Rita asked for Viaticum and the Sacrament of the Sick. She received them in the presence of the community and took the occasion to exhort her Sisters to observe the Rule of the

Order. Then, folding her hands, she asked a blessing from her Abbess. No sooner had she received it than she quietly expired.

It was a Saturday, day of the Virgin. Evening Prayer I of the following Sunday had just begun. Outside, roses were in bloom. Some witnesses conversant with the process of canonization said that several persons had seen her soul ascend in glory.

Be that as it may, we can apply to this holy death a text found in the Song of Songs (3:10; 2:2): "Arise, make haste, My beloved, My dove, My beautiful one, and come. Like a lily among thorns, beautiful is My beloved."

Above the high altar of the basilica in Cascia, a large and beautiful fresco shows St. Rita nestled at the feet of the glorious Christ. It was the moment when she could say: "I am seated in the shadow of the One I desired" (Song of Songs 2:3).

REFLECTION: THE RIGHT IDEA ABOUT DEATH

SAINTS welcome death. If we tremble at the prospect of the great departure to the Beyond, it is precisely because we are not Saints.

In thinking about death, we show how uncertain our faith still is. We ask ourselves what we are going to find on the other side.

Far different is the way of those who, while on earth, have lived for heaven. St. Paul was among them. That is why he could say: "I desire to die and be with Christ" (Philippians 1:23).

St. Bernadette said: "The Blessed Virgin is so beautiful that when we have seen her once, we want to see her again." The reaction of the little seers at Fatima was the same. They asked the "Beautiful Lady" of the apparition to take them back with her to Paradise.

We could apply to these manifestations of faith the antiphon sung at the Easter Vigil: "Like a deer that longs for running streams, my soul longs for You, my God. Athirst is my soul for God, the living God. When shall I go and behold the face of God?" (Psalm 42:2-3).

If we do not want to fear death, we must first make our faith stronger. The best way to do this is to comport ourselves as true Christians and bring about a real conformity between our beliefs and our life. In short, we must create a harmony within ourselves.

Too often there is a kind of discord between our external piety and a life of deep faith. Because we lack this deep faith, we are fearful of death when it begins to show itself. We perceive that we are like the foolish virgins of the Gospel parable and that our lamps are empty (Matthew 25:1-13).

Yet many times we have repeated: "Lord! Lord!" We have multiplied formulas of prayers, novenas, and invocations, and have offered

*candles. However, we have not done the princi-
pal thing—the Father's will in all areas of life.*

*We need to do the Father's will in the matter
of justice and charity, in almsgiving, in purity,
in the forgiving of wrongs, and in the loving
abandonment to Providence.*

*Because we have failed in these matters,
death makes us fearful. But there is still time
to regain our self-control. That is always possible. Let us, then, turn to the Lord in prayer.*

PRAYER: TO PREPARE FOR A GOOD DEATH

D EAR God,
the thought of death frightens me.
And so I come to You with a repentant soul.
I would like to live the rest of my life
with increasing acceptance of death.

I wish very much for an end
like that of Your Saints,
in serenity and joy,
but I have not been much of a Saint so far.
I want with all my heart
to strive to become holy,
at least to some degree.

I sense
that faith must be in proportion to true generosity.
It takes a great deal of faith
to die with joy.

Dear God,
Make my soul truly generous.
Help me to take Your Gospel ever more seri-
    ously
and to make it enter into all the details of my
    life.

By the merits of St. Rita
I beseech You,
dear God,
to deliver me and the ones I love
from the calamity of a sudden death.
May I, on the contrary,
prepare myself in all serenity
for the day that will free me
from the miseries of life.

May I then be united with You
and Your Saints
in the "place of refreshment, light, and peace,"
where all who have showed love on earth
will find each other again forever.
Amen.

FIFTEENTH THURSDAY
Preparatory Prayer, p. 13

LIFE: THE VINE IN FLOWER HAS SPREAD ITS PERFUME

MAY 22, 1457, was, as we have seen, the "true day of birth" of our Saint, the hour of her glorification. Rita had scarcely breathed her last when the prodigies began.

The convent clock was said to have struck three times, though no one had touched it. Rita's "little cell" was filled with an extraordinary light. This brings to mind the "perpetual light" into which the deceased Saint had just entered.

A perfume no less strange also filled the cell, which had until then been permeated with the nauseating odor that was so offensive. The perfume indicated that Rita died "in the odor of sanctity" in the literal as well as the figurative sense.

The fetid wound was suddenly healed. Not only did the oozing stop, but the Stigmata of the thorn became like a precious stone of bright red. "You have placed on [her] head a crown of precious stones," sings the Psalmist (Psalm 21:3).

One of the Sisters of the convent had a paralyzed arm. Her name was Sister Catherine Mancini. Despite this infirmity, she wanted to embrace her companion, who may have been a relative.

She tried to put her arm around the neck of the deceased Rita and succeeded perfectly, having that very moment regained the use of her arm. This was the first miracle obtained by Rita.

While the body was being washed and prepared for burial, the people of Cascia waited impatiently. They wanted to see her whom everybody already was calling "The Saint."

The remains were taken to a chapel of the convent and, so that everyone could see her, the coffin was not closed. This was supposed to be only for a short time, but it lasted 138 years.

A few years after being left open, the coffin was damaged by fire but the body remained intact. "Up to the present," writes Monsignor De Marchi in our day, "and consequently for more than a half millennium, the sentence against the children of Adam has not come about for Rita: 'You are dust and to dust you shall return.' " Her body remains incorrupt.

This preservation is truly exceptional. In 1626, hence more than 150 years after the death, the body was examined. Among other things, the examiner's report noted:

"The white flesh was seen perfectly . . . the eyes with the pupils . . . and the whole face as nicely arranged as a person who died that same day. Also seen were the hands of the said servant of God, white and intact, and the fingers with the nails could be perfectly counted. . . ."

The best historian of St. Rita, Cavallucci, who wrote about the same time—1626—says he can testify that at each opening of the coffin a perfume "like an odoriferous mixture" escaped from it. Moreover, he adds, each time an important grace was obtained through the intercession of the Saint, this perfume was detected by smell inside the convent several days before.

At present, the skin is still intact and well preserved. The face simply appears a little dried up and a little black. The body rests in a glass case placed in a chapel of the new basilica built in 1925.

It should further be noted that—according to oral tradition—on several occasions the Saint has been seen opening her eyes and sometimes turning her head or moving her hands and feet. This is called the "Miracle of the Movements."

At the time of Rita's death there were no official canonizations. It was, so to speak, the voice of the people that declared anyone a Saint. Rita, it can be said, was first beatified by the people, whereupon the bishop of Spoleto authorized her veneration. The first church intended specifically for placement of the Saint's body was built in the late sixteenth century.

Before long, May 22 became, so to speak, a national holiday of Italy. The official beatification was made by Urban VIII in 1628, and the canonization by Leo XIII in 1900. Since this latter date—1900—veneration of St. Rita has grown wonderfully throughout the world.

REFLECTION: THE SCHOOL
OF THE SAINTS

*I*N *1957 the unforgettable festivities of the fifth centenary of the Saint's death took place in Cascia. The year before, Pope Pius XII sent, for this occasion, a magnificent letter to the very Reverend Superior General of the Augustinians.*

In his letter the Sovereign Pontiff held up St. Rita as model for the whole world because, he wrote, in her life are found examples for all situations. She was a young girl, a wife, mother, widow, and nun. She faced and overcame the trials that can afflict a human existence in all these states of life.

Such a life deserves to be studied and imitated, but the emphasis should be on imitation. Our Saints, that is, ought not to be mere subjects of admiring curiosity.

Nor should they be seen primarily as "miracle workers." They are not "sorcerers of heaven" (title of a film on the Curé of Ars), or supernatural beings who have to be made favorable toward us and whom we honor mostly because of personal interest.

In reality, our Saints are, before all else, "Witnesses of God." Their life shows what the Lord's grace can bring about in a soul that does not try to flee such grace.

What the Saints have done we can do, even if the circumstances are different. We have at our disposal the same Divine gifts and the same means.

It is simply a matter of having the courage to use the gifts and the means. Above all the rest, courage is what we should ask for from our Saints.

We should approach them as good pupils in their school, not as beggars who only ask for material favors.

If we are good pupils in the School of the Saints, would that not be the best means of making them favorable toward us? Then the school would enjoy the admirable "Communion of Saints."

On the strength of this Communion, people in heaven help their needy brothers and sisters on earth to come and join them, and people on earth congratulate their glorious brothers and sisters and strive to come and be with them, in perpetual light and perfect joy.

PRAYER: TO IMITATE ST. RITA IN BEARING WITNESS TO CHRIST

A S we come,
dear God,
to the end of the story of a Saint loved by all,
we want first to thank You.
Amid the troubled times in which we live,
St. Rita's life has given us hope and courage.
She has shown us
that human beings can practice virtues
and gain merit.

Because of St. Rita we begin to see,
dear God,
a little more of the mystery of Your Church.
We have been taught
that Your Church is nothing less than Your Son
continuing His Incarnation
in the history of the world.

We have also been taught,
dear God,
that all of us are members
of Your Son's Mystical Body.
Sometimes, in the past, it has been difficult for
us
to believe in this magnificent truth of our
Creed.
The reason was
that we considered only ourselves
with our sins, our meanness, our tepidity.
We told ourselves we were not fit
to be members of Christ's Mystical Body.

Then, dear God,
we discovered in our Sister Rita
a wonderful reflection of Your Word made
    flesh.
Like Him, she had no other will than Yours
and no other love than the love that reigns
among the three Divine Persons
and shines upon the world.

We have seen her good and gentle
even when she was so badly treated in return.
We have seen her patient,
solely preoccupied with the salvation of her
    dear ones.

We have seen her helpful to the disinherited
and becoming poor solely to be enriched
by the supernatural riches of Christ.
Her life consisted in modeling herself on Him.
She was truly
what every baptized person should be:
another Christ.

Having seen what she did and what she was,
we now understand that Christians like her
are truly the kind of members Christ seeks
in order to form His Church,
which is His Mystical Body.
Through St. Rita, we humbly ask of You, dear
    God,
that, like her, each of us may be a useful mem-
    ber
of Your Church

and continue here on earth the Incarnation of
Your Son.
We further ask of You
that, like her, we may manifest to the world
the tender mercy of Jesus.

PRAYER TO ST. RITA

O St. Rita,
help us and all the ones we love
to accomplish the plan of Love
that God desires for each one of us.
Amen.

St. Rita pictured with the Crown of Thorns
to signify the Stigmata that she bore.

NOVENAS, TRIDUUMS, AND PRAYERS TO ST. RITA

REASONS WHY OUR PRAYERS ARE PLEASING TO THE LORD

OUR life is in the hands of God, notwithstanding that we often suffer in our body and in our soul because of our sins. What more normal than to address ourselves to our Father for the purpose of being delivered from what we are suffering? And since St. Rita is a friend of both God and ourselves, she makes intercession for us.

1. Praying with Confidence

"Put away all anxiety from your minds. Present your needs to God in every form of prayer and in petitions filled with gratitude. Then God's own peace, which surpasses all understanding, will stand guard over your hearts and minds, in Christ Jesus" (Philippians 4:6-7).

2. Going to Confession, if Necessary, and Receiving Holy Communion

"Beloved, if our hearts do not condemn us, we can be sure that God is with us and that we will receive from His hands whatever we ask. For we are keeping His commandments and doing what is pleasing to Him" (1 John 3:21-22).

3. Committing Oneself to a Christian Life

"Since you have been raised with Christ, set your hearts on what pertains to things above, where Christ is seated at God's right hand. Mind things above rather than things of earth. For you have died! Your life is hidden now with Christ in God" (Colossians 3:1-3).

4. Dialoguing Humbly with God through St. Rita in an Effort to Understand God's Mysterious Will

"And now, brothers, I beg you through the mercy of God to offer your bodies as a living sacrifice holy and pleasing to God—your spiritual worship. Do not conform yourselves to this world but be transformed by the renewal of your mind. Then you will be able to judge what is God's will what is good, pleasing, and perfect" (Romans 12:1-2).

NOVENA TO ST. RITA

THE WORD OF GOD

"I have come to set a man against his father, a daughter against her mother. Your enemies will be the members of your own household."
—Matthew 10:35-36

"As long as you remain in Me and I in you, you bear much fruit, but apart from Me you can do nothing."   —John 15:5

"I do not wish to boast of anything but the Cross of our Lord Jesus Christ. Through it, the world has been crucified to me and I to the world."   —Galatians 6:14

NOVENA PRAYERS

Prayer to the Heavenly Father

HEAVENLY Father, rewarder of the humble, You blessed St. Rita with charity and patience. You kept her faithful to the pattern of poverty and humility of Your Son during the years of her married life and especially in the convent where she served You for the rest of her life.

In St. Rita You give us an example of the Gospel lived to perfection, for You called her to seek Your Kingdom in this world by striving to live in perfect charity. In her life You teach us that the commandments of heaven are summarized in love of You and love of others.

May the prayers of St. Rita help me and her example inspire me to carry my cross and to love You always. Pour upon me the spirit of wisdom and love with which You filled Your servant, so that I may serve You faithfully and reach eternal life. I ask this through Christ our Lord. Amen.

Novena Prayer

ST. Rita, God gave you to us as an example of charity and patience, and offered you a share in the Passion of His Son. I thank Him for the many blessings He bestowed upon you during your lifetime, especially during your unhappy marriage and during the illness you suffered in the convent.

May your example encourage me to carry my own Cross patiently and to live a holier life. By serving God as you did, may I please Him with my faith and my actions.

I fail because of my weakness. Pray to God for me that He may restore me to His love through His grace and help me on my way to salvation.

In your kindness hear my prayer and ask God to grant me this particular request if it be His will: *(Mention your request)*.

May your prayers help me to live in fidelity to my calling as you did and bring me to the deeper love of God and my neighbor until I reach eternal life in heaven. Amen.

Alternative Novena Prayer

ST. Rita, from your childhood till your death you tried to conceal from the world your deep humility and your eminent virtues and to keep yourself hidden with Christ in God. This saintly mode of life was the reason for your elevation to the exalted glory that you now enjoy in heaven.

But your loving Jesus, Whose humility you perfectly imitated, desired to glorify you also on earth. Scarcely had your beautiful soul entered paradise than many miracles were wrought through your intercession while simultaneously people from near and far proclaimed you a Saint. And in due time, you were declared a Saint by the voice of the Supreme Shepherd of the Church.

Now, devotion to you has spread throughout the world, and more than any other Saint you enjoy the privilege of being called the "Saint of the Impossible" and "Advocate of the Most Hopeless Cases." O glorious St. Rita, what case is more desperate than ours, poor creatures that we are, blinded by pride, the sin most offensive to God and to yourself!

Dear Saint, obtain for us from God the inestimable favor of knowing we have nothing to be proud of, and that without Him we are nothing and can do nothing. Preserve us by your powerful intercession from the eternal ruin into which the proud and rebellious angels fell, so that one day we may be permitted to share the glory that you, most humble Saint, enjoy—a glory granted only to the humble. Amen.

Concluding Prayer

O GOD, You were pleased to bestow upon St. Rita such great grace that she imitated Your example in the love of enemies and bore in her heart and on her forehead the sacred marks of Your love and Passion.

By her merits and intercession, grant that we may love our enemies and ever contemplate with deep contrition the sorrows of Your Passion. For You live forever and ever. Amen.

ALTERNATIVE NOVENA TO ST. RITA

Supplications

HOLY Patroness of those in need, St. Rita, your pleadings before your Divine Lord are irresistible. For your lavishness in granting favors you have been called the "Advocate of the Hopeless" and even of the "Impossible."

You are so humble, so mortified, so patient, and so compassionate in love for your crucified Jesus that you can obtain from Him anything you ask. Therefore, all confidently have recourse to you in the hope of comfort or relief.

Be propitious toward your suppliants and show your power with God in their behalf. Be lavish with your favors now as you have been in so many wonderful cases for the greater glory of God, the spread of your devotion, and the consolation of those who trust in you.

We promise, if our petition be granted, to glorify you by making known your favor, and to bless you and sing your praises forever. Relying then on your merits and power before the Sacred Heart of Jesus, we ask of you *(Mention your request)*.

Prayer of Intercession

BY the singular merits of your childhood, *obtain our request for us (repeated after each invocation)*.

By your perfect union with the Divine will,

By your heroic suffering during your married life,

By the consolation you experienced at the conversion of your husband,

By the anguish that filled your heart at the murder of your husband,

By your sacrifice of your children rather than see them grievously offend God,

By your miraculous entrance into the convent,

By your severe penance and thrice daily bloody scourging,

By your suffering from the wound received from the thorn of your Crucified Savior,

By the Divine love that consumed your heart,

By your remarkable devotion to the Blessed Sacrament on which alone you subsisted for years,

By the happiness with which you parted from your trials to join your Divine Spouse,

By the perfect example you gave to people of every state of life,

Pray for us, St. Rita.

—*That we may be worthy of the promises of Christ.*

Concluding Prayer

O GOD, in Your infinite tenderness You have been pleased to regard the prayer of Your servant Rita, and to grant to her supplication that which is impossible to human foresight, skill, and effort, in reward for her compassionate love and firm reliance on Your promises.

Have pity on our adversities and comfort us in our calamities, that unbelievers may know that You are the recompense of the humble, the defense of the helpless, and the strength of those who trust in You. Grant this in the Name of Jesus the Lord. Amen.

SHORT NOVENA TO ST. RITA

Recite the following prayers for nine successive days.

1st, 4th, and 7th Day

MOST compassionate St. Rita, Advocate of Desperate Cases, consider with benevolence the prayers of an anguished heart and please obtain for me the grace that I need so much.

Our Father, Hail Mary, Glory Be.

2nd, 5th, and 8th Day

MOST compassionate St. Rita, Advocate of Desperate Cases, I have recourse to you because I am certain of the power of your intercession. Please receive my request and present it to God yourself.

Our Father, Hail Mary, Glory Be.

3rd, 6th, and 9th Day

MOST compassionate St. Rita, last recourse in urgent cases, I entrust myself to you with faith and love. In the situation that I have explained to you, you are my ultimate refuge. Have pity on me, through the Passion of Christ in which you shared so intimately!

Our Father, Hail Mary, Glory Be.

TRIDUUM IN HONOR OF ST. RITA: TO OBTAIN A GRACE

First Day

O GLORIOUS St. Rita, you were favored on earth with gifts from heaven to be used for the benefit of others. Now you have become an all-powerful Protectress in heaven. Help abundantly people who are suffering.

Here is a soul that has recourse to you with trust and surrender. The grace it asks of you is the most ardent desire of its heart. It would like to express the desire with words of faith and by prayer. But its prayer is too halting.

Intercede, if you please, for this soul, since the Lord has shown in a visible way that He listens to and grants your prayer.

Glory be to the Father. . . .

Second Day

I RETURN with an impatient heart to beseech you, O glorious St. Rita, whom the Lord has made the dispenser of the rarest favors.

Charity, O St. Rita, set your heart aflame for the sake of the poor and afflicted. This charity has been made known to the world by the splendor of your favors. Like a magnet, it attracts to your altar a multitude of souls tormented by doubt and racked with pain.

You also experienced pain: feelings of pain within the family circle, in the sad days of your widowhood. Because of this experience, O dear Saint, you can console all hearts who recommend themselves to you in their pain. They are not as steadfast in faith as you were in your painful days. Bring them consolation, lest they despair and forget God.

Glory be to the Father. . . .

Third Day

O GLORIOUS St. Rita, it is my wretchedness, my trust in your intercession, and the expectation of being heard that hasten me to the foot of your altar. The greatest obstacle to receiving Divine favors is sin, but I am contrite. It is my wish that you yourself present to God the homage of my repentant heart.

If the grace of forgiveness that irradiates my soul does not yet make it worthy of the favors I ask, well then, because of the merits of the Divine Heart of Jesus and of His most gentle Mother, and because of your merits, I am confident of being heard.

I subordinate the graces I ask of you, dear Saint, to the eternal good of my soul.

And above all else, may God's will ever be done in me, to His greater glory. Amen.

Glory be to the Father. . . .

TRIDUUM IN HONOR OF ST. RITA: FOR THE SICK

First Day

ALL-POWERFUL God, You are a benevolent and loving Father. Look on these sick people, who ask You for a return to health. May Your infinite goodness and Your mercy be activated in view of the merits of Your most faithful Spouse St. Rita. We put these sick under her protection.

The Saint of Cascia practiced heroic virtues. She also practiced the admirable charity that impelled her to help the poor sick.

In recognition of these virtues and especially of this charity, come, O Lord, and help the sick recommended to You. Restore their health, for the sake of Your glory, and for the sake of Your beloved Servant's glory, the Saint of Cascia.

AND you, St. Rita, help us, you who are so close to God. We have put our trust in your intercession. Reward our hopes, hear our prayers.

Glory be to the Father. . . .

Second Day

O MOST gentle Heart of Jesus, faith and love dictated to Martha and Mary this message: "Lord, the one You love is sick." With the same faith and love we also address these words to You, because we feel the need of Your help and Your mercy.

May Your grace, O Jesus, come through the intercession of Your beloved St. Rita, so that the sick we recommend to You may regain their health.

Grant our request through the merits of this Saint, her penances, and the dreadful sorrow she endured in the fifteen years when she shared in Your sorrowful Passion.

ADDRESS, O St. Rita, a prayer to your crucified Spouse. He certainly will hearken to you and grant health to these sick, who have put their trust in you.

O kind St. Rita, it is because of your mediation that we expect this favor; and, as we are certain that God inspires in us this prayer to you, so we are certain, because of your merits, of being heard.

Glory be to the Father. . . .

Third Day

O DIVINE heart of Jesus, Your life on earth was an act of boundless love and mercy for a suffering world. Deign to look upon these sick. They trust in You and ask You for bodily health, if such health is necessary for the salvation of their soul.

You know, O Jesus, how much these people are suffering on their bed of pain. If You so desire, You can save them. You saved many people broken by all sorts of diseases.

Lord, if we are not worthy of being heard, we beg the support of Your beloved St. Rita. Through her You have been pleased, so often, to dispense the treasures of Your mercy.

AND you, St. Rita, pray to the gentle Jesus. Pray to Him for us and for these sick, who have complete trust in your protection.

Do this, dear Saint, on account of the merits acquired in your last four years through sufferings brought upon you by a dreadful mysterious malady that took you to Paradise.

In consideration of these merits, obtain from the Lord fulfillment of our desire: the bodily health of the people recommended to you, so they may thank you and as soon as possible do the works their sanctification requires.

Glory be to the Father. . . .

TRIDUUM IN HONOR OF ST. RITA:
TO GIVE THANKS

First Day

O EVER-LIVING God, Your mercy is bound-less and Your goodness immeasurable.
Here, before Your Divine Majesty, I lie pros-trate to give You thanks for having granted me
through the merits of St. Rita what I asked
from You.

I confess, O my God, that I was unworthy of
Your favors, but You, ever generous and good,
heard the prayers of this Saint and granted me
what I really did not deserve.

O St. Rita, how great is my gratitude to you!
I can find no words to express the feelings
of my heart.

O you, who are so good, St. Rita, to people
who have recourse to your heavenly protection,
grant that I may become continually ever more
worthy of God's mercy and your protection.

Glory be to the Father. . . .

Second Day

O MOST holy Heart of Jesus, to show
Yourself generous to people who call
upon You, You said through the Prophet that
You do not wish the death of the sinner but his
conversion and his life. I acknowledge a singu-lar act of Your boundless charity in granting

the grace so much desired, through the intercession of St. Rita.

And what could I return to You, O Lord, for all You have accorded me?

TO you, St. Rita, my heavenly patron, to you, after God, I owe the grace of having been heard. Therefore, I ask of you another favor: it is that you yourself, so close to the Lord, thank Him in my behalf for the grace received.

Obtain from God something else for me: it is that the gratitude I feel toward Him and toward you may remain forever in my heart.

Also obtain for me the grace never again to offend a Father so generous and the grace to grow in love for Him until I can love Him in heaven.

Glory be to the Father. . . .

Third Day

O GOOD Jesus, in You gratitude to the Father dwells everlastingly. For, by means of striking prodigies, He made You known and glorified You in the world: in a world which, full of ingratitude and not wanting to know You, heaped reproaches upon You.

Here, in Your presence, good Jesus, is one whom You heard because of the intercession of St. Rita and who now wants to thank You.

O St. Rita, how happy I am to praise you by a name that shows your power with God.

Oh how much I would like all people to know you, St. Rita, and venerate you. Oh how much I would like them to experience the comfort and help of your heavenly patronage in the tribulations of life.

O St. Rita, in return for the blessings I have received from God through your intercession, I will make myself the indefatigable propagator of your name and of devotion to you amid the faithful.

To all I will declare that you are truly the Saint of impossible cases, the Advocate very much heard by God, especially the Advocate for the unfortunate souls who have no more hope on earth. Amen.

Glory be to the Father. . . .

PRAYER IN DIFFICULT AND
DESPERATE CASES

O POWERFUL and glorious St. Rita, here at your feet is a disconsolate soul who, having need of help, has recourse to you with the fond hope of being heard.

Because of my unworthiness and my past infidelities, I dare not hope my prayers will succeed in gaining God's mercy. That is why I feel the need of an all-powerful mediatrix. It is you I have looked for, St. Rita, as the incomparable Saint of impossible and desperate cases.

O dear Saint, take my cause to heart. Intercede with God so that I may obtain the grace I need so much and ardently desire *(Mention the desired grace)*.

Do not, dear Saint, let me leave your presence without having been heard. If something in me is an obstacle to obtaining the grace I ask, help me remove it.

Infuse my prayer with your precious merits and present it to your heavenly Spouse together with your prayer. Thus enriched by you, kind Rita, my prayer will be heard. You were the wife most faithful, and you felt the sorrows of your heavenly Spouse in His Passion. How could He reject a prayer enriched by you or not hear it?

All my trust is in you. Relying on your mediation, I await with a tranquil heart the fulfillment of my request.

O dear St. Rita, may the trust and hope I place in you not be lessened. Grant that my request be not in vain; then I shall make known to everyone the goodness of your heart and the great power of your intercession. Amen.

AND You, dear Jesus, Whose adorable Heart always showed You so sensitive to the slightest misery of people, be moved by my needs. Disregard my failings and unworthiness. Grant me, O Jesus, the grace that I so greatly desire and that, for me and with me, Your faithful spouse, St. Rita, asks of You.

Yes, good Jesus, for the sake of the faithfulness with which St. Rita always responded to Divine grace; for the sake of all the gifts with which You have wanted to fill her soul; for the sake of all she suffered in her life as wife, mother, and participant in Your sorrowful Passion; and, in conclusion, for the sake of the extraordinary power of intercession with which You have wanted to reward her faithfulness, grant me the grace so necessary for me. Amen.

AND you, Virgin Mary, you are our good Mother in heaven. You are the depositary of the Divine treasures and the dispenser of all graces. Add your powerful intercession to that of your great devotee St. Rita, to obtain from God the grace so much desired by me. Amen.

PRAYER OF THANKSGIVING

IT is with a heart filled with gratitude that today I come to you, O glorious and powerful St. Rita.

In the hour of danger, at a time when my happiness and the happiness of the ones dear to me were threatened, I implored your aid, as my soul was distressed and filled with apprehension.

I besought you, O glorious St. Rita, you whom everybody calls Saint of the Impossible, Advocate in desperate cases, and Refuge in the final hour. My trust in you was not disappointed.

I return to you, no longer with tears of suffering in my eyes but with joy and serenity in the heart. I return to present to you my boundless gratitude.

This joy and serenity I owe to you, dear Saint, to you who interceded with God on my behalf despite my unworthiness and obtained the grace I desired.

For this grace I am thankful to you, O consoler of the afflicted. Speech fails me, however, when I try to find words to express my gratitude. I can only murmur: Thank you . . . Thank you . . . Thank you . . . St. Rita.

Then, to show you in a more appropriate way how boundless is my gratitude, I promise to spread with ever more zeal knowledge of the

Fifteen Thursdays. I also promise to make you loved by people who still do not know you and have not, like me, experienced your immeasurable kindness.

I further promise, dear Saint, to do my best to spread the devotion of the Fifteen Thursdays and as often as possible to attend Masses celebrated in your honor.

To make myself ever more worthy of help from heaven and of your saintly protection, I take the resolution from this day forward to carry out my Christian duties more conscientiously and more fervently.

O dear St. Rita, to you I entrust the care of presenting to God my sincere resolution and thanking Him in my behalf for the grace liberally granted.

In your kindness never forsake me and always keep me under your saintly and active protection. After having benefited by it on earth, may I meet you again in heaven to express more appropriately all my gratitude to you. Amen.

SUPPLICATION TO ST. RITA
For the Day of Her Feast (May 22)

O GLORIOUS St. Rita, my patron, here I am at your feet on this day when, everywhere on earth, so many praises are sung to your name. Besides the prayers that are rising up to you from all corners of the world, hear also this humble and trustful prayer that comes from the depths of my heart and ascends to your presence in heaven.

Also deign to look favorably upon me, and intercede with God for me so that I may obtain at this moment the grace necessary for me.

I promise you to follow ever faithfully your noble examples of Christian virtue and to sing the praises of your name all the days of my life.

Bless my family, and turn all evil away from us by keeping us united with the Lord and faithful to His sacred precepts.

Intercede for the Sovereign Pontiff, for the priests of this diocese, and for all priests and all Catholic people.

In consideration of your eminent merits, may God bring peace to our troubled times, and may the Church of Christ be victorious over all doctrinal error so that soon there will be on earth one flock and one shepherd.

Our Father. Hail Mary. Glory be to the Father *(three times)*.

St. Rita of Cascia, pray for us.

LITANY OF ST. RITA

(For Private Devotion)

LORD, have mercy.
Christ, have mercy.
Lord, have mercy.
Christ, hear us.
Christ, graciously hear us.
God the Father of heaven,
have mercy on us.
God the Son, Redeemer of
the world, *have mercy on
us.*
God the Holy Spirit, *have
mercy on us.*
Holy Trinity, one God,
have mercy on us.
Immaculate Mary, Mother
of God, *pray for us.*
Mary, Mother and support
of the unfortunate,
Mary, Queen of all Saints,
St. Rita, our advocate,
St. Rita, enamored of soli-
tude,
St. Rita, model of purity,
St. Rita, example of kind-
ness,
St. Rita, mirror of obedi-
ence,
St. Rita, model of wife and
mother,
St. Rita, of inexhaustible
patience,
St. Rita, astonishing in for-
titude,
St. Rita, heroic in sacri-
fice,
St. Rita, generous in for-
giving,
St. Rita, martyr in peni-
tence,
St. Rita, benefactress of
the poor,
St. Rita, submissive to the
Divine call
St. Rita, mirror of conven-
tual life,
St. Rita, miracle of mortifi-
cation,
St. Rita, adorer of Jesus
Crucified,
St. Rita, pierced by a thorn
of Jesus,
St. Rita, pearl of Paradise,
St. Rita, pride of the
Augustinian Order,
St. Rita, precious stone of
Umbria,
St. Rita, with very influen-
tial power of intercession,
St. Rita, charitable star of
the straying,
St. Rita, assured comfort of
the afflicted,
St. Rita, Saint of the
Impossible,
St. Rita, Advocate in des-
perate cases,

Pray for us is repeated after each invocation.

St. Rita, powerful help of all who call upon you,

Lamb of God, You take away the sins of the world; *spare us, O Lord.*

Lamb of God, You take away the sins of the world; *graciously hear us, O Lord.*

Lamb of God, You take away the sins of the world; *have mercy on us.*

℣. Pray for us, St. Rita.

℟. *That we may be made worthy of the promises of Christ.*

O MOST merciful God, You made St. Rita renowned by the favor of continual prodigies. Grant that by her merits we may obtain all the graces we ask of You with faith. We ask this through our Lord, Jesus Christ. ℟. *Amen.*

PRAYER FOR A PARTICULAR GRACE

O St. Rita, Saint of the Impossible and Advocate of Desperate Cases, I have recourse to you since I am engulfed by a trial.

Free my poor heart from the anguish that oppresses it and restore peace to my troubled spirit. You whom God has established as the Advocate of Desperate Cases, obtain for me the grace that I ask of you *(mention it here)*. Shall I be the only one not to experience the efficacy of your powerful intercession?

If my sins constitute an obstacle to the fulfillment of my most cherished wishes, obtain for me the great grace of a sincere repentance and pardon through a good Confession. In any case, do not allow me to continue to live in such great affliction. Have pity on me!

O LORD, see the hope that I have in You! Listen to Your Blessed Rita who intercedes for us, the afflicted who are humanly without hope. Hear her prayers once more by manifesting Your mercy to us. Amen.

PRAYER FOR A SICK PERSON

MOST dear Heart of Jesus, with the same faith and the same love that dictated to Martha and Mary this appeal to You: "Lord, the one You love is sick!" I also dare to direct these words to You, for I ardently hope for the help of Your Divine mercy.

May Your grace, Lord Jesus, come through the hands of Your Most Holy Mother Mary and of Your servant Rita, so that the sick person whom I recommend may be brought back to health. Grant me this grace, O Lord, by the merits of Your faithful Rita. See her penances and her great pains that she suffered for fifteen years by which You wished to unite her in a special way to Your Passion.

O St. Rita, intercede for me with your crucified Spouse. May He grant health to this sick person for whom I pray to you. It is through your special mediation that I await this grace. Convinced that it is God Himself Who inspires me to pray to you, I am certain that, through your merits, He will hear me in one manner or another for His greater glory. I believe it, I hope it, I am sure of it. I thank you in advance.

Glory be to the Father, and to the Son, and to the Holy Spirit. As it was in the beginning, is now, and ever shall be, world without end. Amen.

ST. RITA'S ROSES

*T*HE custom of blessing and distributing roses on the Feast Day of St. Rita (May 22) commemorates the miraculous blooming of a rose in the garden of St. Rita's home in January on snow-covered ground. It also commemorates the heavenly odor that emanates from the body of the Saint, especially at times when she is particularly lavish with her favors. The Holy See, having been so impressed by this wonderful occurrence caused it to be thoroughly investigated and finally accepted it as one of the three miracles required, at that time, for the canonization of the Saint, thereby establishing its authenticity beyond question.

PRAYER OF THE ROSES

O BLESSED St. Rita, my powerful advocate, behold me prostrate before your Divine Spouse, Jesus, your Lord, your God, and your All. Behold me recalling His favors to you, that you may plead for me.

May this blessed Rose, sweet with the memories of your daily acts of love before the image of the Crucified Savior, and of the wonders wrought for you in your dying moments, give me confidence that you in heaven will plead that I, too, may share in the good things God has in store for your clients. *"St. Rita, mystical Rose of every virtue, pray for us."*

APPENDIX: MASS OF ST. RITA

Entrance Antiphon

Galatians 6:14

*M*Y *only glory is the Cross of our Lord Jesus Christ, which crucifies the world to me and me to the world.*

Opening Prayer

*F*ATHER in heaven,
  You granted to St. Rita
a share in the passion of Your Son.
Give us courage and strength in time of trial,
so that by our patient endurance
we may enter more deeply
into the Paschal Mystery of Your Son,
Who lives and reigns with You and the Holy
  Spirit,
one God, for ever and ever.
℟. *Amen.*

Reading I

Proverbs 2:1-15

A reading from the book of Proverbs

*Rita was seriously attached to the education
of her children.*

*M*Y son, if you receive my words
  and treasure my commands,
Turning your ear to wisdom,
  inclining your heart to understanding;
Yes, if you call to intelligence,
  and to understanding raise your voice;

121

If you seek her like silver,
    and like hidden treasures search her out:

Then will you understand the fear of the Lord;
    the knowledge of God you will find;
For the Lord gives wisdom,
    from His mouth come knowledge and under-
        standing;
He has counsel in store for the upright,
    He is the shield of those who walk honestly,
Guarding the paths of justice,
    protecting the way of His pious ones.

Then you will understand rectitude and justice,
    honesty, every good path;
For wisdom will enter your heart,
    knowledge will please your soul,
Discretion will watch over you,
    understanding will guard you;

Saving you from the way of evil men,
    from men of perverse speech,
Who leave the straight paths
    to walk in ways of darkness,
Who delight in doing evil,
    rejoice in perversity;
Whose ways are crooked,
    and devious their paths.
The Word of the Lord. ℟. *Thanks be to God.*

Responsorial Psalm   Psalm 27:1, 3, 4, 5, 11, 13

℟. *Be strong; hope in the Lord.*

THE Lord is my light and my salvation;
  whom should I fear?
The Lord is my life's refuge;
  of whom should I be afraid?—R̰.

Though an army encamp against me,
  my heart will not fear;
Though war be waged upon me,
  even then will I trust.—R̰.

One thing I ask of the Lord;
  this I seek:
To dwell in the house of the Lord
  all the days of my life,
That I may gaze on the loveliness of the Lord
  and contemplate His temple.—R̰.

For He will hide me in His abode
  in the day of trouble;
He will conceal me in the shelter of His tent,
  He will set me high upon a rock.—R̰.

Show me, O Lord, Your way,
  and lead me on a level path,
  because of my adversaries.—R̰.

I believe that I shall see the bounty of the Lord
  in the land of the living.—R̰.

Reading II   Romans 12:9-21

A reading from the letter of Paul to the Romans

Do not be conquered by evil, but conquer evil
with good.

YOUR love must be sincere. Detest what is
  evil, cling to what is good. Love one anoth-

er with the affection of brothers. Anticipate each other in showing respect.

Do not grow slack but be fervent in spirit; He Whom you serve is the Lord. Rejoice in hope, be patient under trial, persevere in prayer. Look on the needs of the saints as your own; be generous in offering hospitality. Bless your persecutors; bless and do not curse them. Rejoice with those who rejoice, weep with those who weep. Have the same attitude toward all. Put away ambitious thoughts and associate with those who are lowly. Do not be wise in your own estimation.

Never repay injury with injury. See that your conduct is honorable in the eyes of all. If possible, live peaceably with everyone.

Beloved, do not avenge yourselves; leave that to God's wrath, for it is written: " 'Vengeance is mine; I will repay,' says the Lord." But "if your enemy is hungry, feed him; if he is thirsty, give him something to drink; by doing this you will heap burning coals upon his head." Do not be conquered by evil but conquer evil with good.—The Word of the Lord. ℟. *Thanks be to God.*

Alleluia   1 John 4:16b

℟. *Alleluia.*

G OD is love,
and he who abides in love abides in God,
and God in him.
℟. *Alleluia.*

Gospel John 15:1-14

℣. The Lord be with you. ℟. *And also with you.*
✦ A reading from the holy gospel according to
John. ℟. *Glory to you, Lord.*

As the Father has loved Me, so have I loved
you. Live on in My love.

JESUS said to His disciples:
"I am the true vine
and My Father is the vinegrower.
He prunes away
every barren branch,
but the fruitful ones
He trims clean
to increase their yield.

"You are clean already,
thanks to the word I have spoken to you.
Live on in Me, as I do in you.
No more than a branch can bear fruit of itself,
apart from the vine,
can you bear fruit
apart from Me.

"I am the vine, you are the branches.
He who lives in Me and I in him,
will produce abundantly,
for apart from Me you can do nothing.
A man who does not live in Me
is like a withered, rejected branch,
picked up to be thrown in the fire and burnt.

"If you live in Me,
and My words stay part of you

you may ask what you will—
it will be done for you.
My Father has been glorified
in your bearing much fruit
and becoming My disciples.

"As the Father has loved Me,
so I have loved you.
Live on in My love.
You will live in My love
if you keep My commandments,
even as I have kept My Father's command-
    ments,
and live in His love.

"All this I tell you
that My joy may be yours
and your joy may be complete.
This is My commandment:
love one another
as I have loved you.

"There is no greater love than this:
to lay down one's life for one's friends.
You are My friends
if you do what I command you."
The gospel of the Lord. ℟. *Praise to You, Lord
    Jesus Christ.*

Prayer Over the Gifts

L ORD,
    through the prayers of St. Rita
touch our hearts with compassion
for the sufferings of Your Son.

Free us from all sin,
that we may offer You this sacrifice of praise
in holiness of heart.
We ask this through Christ our Lord.
℟. *Amen.*

Preface

℣. The Lord be with you. ℟. *And also with you.*
℣. Lift up your hearts. ℟. *We lift them up to the*
Lord. ℣. Let us give thanks to the Lord our
God. ℟. *It is right to give Him thanks and*
praise.

FATHER, all-powerful and ever-living God,
we do well always and everywhere to give
You thanks.
In the person of St. Rita
You show us a wonderful example.
She teaches us how to love You, Father,
and in loving You
to love all Your children.

Love was her strength,
love the great impulse of her life
at every stage of her pilgrimage,
as she kept before her eyes
the redeeming Passion of Your Son.

She has given us a pattern
of penance and charity,
caught up to the heights of joy
by the rapture of love,
which leads by way of the Cross
to the joyful light of the resurrection.

With angels and archangels
and all the choirs of heaven
we sing in praise of Your glory:

Holy, holy, holy Lord, God of power and might,
heaven and earth are full of Your glory.
    Hosanna in the highest.
Blessed is He Who comes in the name of the
        Lord.
    Hosanna in the highest.

Communion Antiphon   John 15:5

*T*HEY who live in Me, and I in them, will
  bear much fruit, says the Lord, alleluia.

Prayer After Communion

*L*ORD,
  You have shared with us the joys of heaven
in this holy meal.
Inspired by the example of St. Rita
may we bear always in our hearts
the imprint of Your redeeming love,
and so gain the reward of everlasting peace,
in the kingdom where You live and reign for
    ever and ever.
℟. *Amen.*